YOUR BIBLE

By the Same Author

YOUR BIBLE

LOUIS CASSELS

FUNK & WAGNALLS

Maps by Stephen Kraft

The Scripture quotations in this publication are from the Revised Standard Version of the Bible, copyrighted 1946 and 1952 by the Division of Christian Education, National Council of Churches, and used by permission.

COPYRIGHT © 1966, 1967 BY LOUIS CASSELS

LIBRARY OF CONGRESS CATALOG CARD NUMBER: 67-11197

FIRST PAPERBOUND EDITION PUBLISHED IN 1969
BY ARRANGEMENT WITH DOUBLEDAY & CO.

FUNK & WAGNALLS, *A Division of* READER'S DIGEST BOOKS, INC.

PRINTED IN THE UNITED STATES OF AMERICA

To Molly and Mike

ACKNOWLEDGMENTS

The author wishes to record his great debt and profound gratitude to two good Christian women whose contribution to this book was made in full expectation of total anonymity.

Mrs. Frank Lyman not only typed the manuscript, but also applied to it, as it went through the mill, the expert critical judgment of a veteran Sunday School teacher. Her comments and suggestions were invaluable.

Mrs. Louis Cassels not only saw to the care, feeding, and encouragement of the author, but also served as a discerning first reader. Her role is aptly summarized in Proverbs 31:10–12.

L.C.

CONTENTS

MAPS

FOR WHOM THIS BOOK WAS WRITTEN

This book is for people who want to get acquainted with the Bible and who are starting pretty much from scratch.

I've encountered many such during the years that I've been writing a syndicated newspaper column on religion. Among them have been Protestants and Catholics, men and women, teen-agers and adults. Some already are convinced Christians; others still are seeking a faith to live by. Some rarely or never go to church; others are very active in church life. The one thing they all have in common is a guilty feeling about the Bible. They are satisfied that they *ought* to read it, but either they have never gotten around to it, or they have tried it only to wind up confused and repelled rather than enlightened.

If you've made previous attempts at Bible reading with unhappy results, you may rest assured that this is no reflection on your intelligence or spiritual depth. For the reader who plows into it without adequate preparation, the Bible can be a roadblock rather than a pathway to faith. I once had a friend who embarked with great determination on a Bible-reading project. He began at the beginning, which may seem quite logical but which is in fact a singularly unfortunate place to start reading the Bible. He found himself confronted at the outset with a story of creation which he assumed he was supposed to accept as literal cosmology and which seemed to be in direct conflict with all that he knew about modern scientific concepts of evolution. He continued reading, with mounting incredulity, about a snake that talked; about men who begat children after they were five hundred years old; and about a boat that was big enough to hold one pair each of all species of creatures on earth. He persevered until he reached a passage that said God once made the sun stand still in order to give the Israelites more daylight in which to complete the slaughter of an enemy army. Here he finally balked. He could not reconcile a bloodthirsty war-god with the loving, merciful Father in Heaven revealed by Jesus Christ.

"I've given up Bible reading," he told me. "I found it was undermining my faith."

I'm sure his experience was not unique. But it doesn't have to be that way. Reading the Bible *can* be the best thing that ever happened to you. It can enable you to grow, in one of its own great phrases, "in the knowledge and love of God." It can be "a light for your pathway" through every stage of life. It can lift up your heart when you're in deep trouble, and it can prick you awake when you're drifting along in self-satisfied complacency. In the most profound sense, it can make a new person of you.

It will do these things for you if you'll take the trouble —and it really isn't a great deal of trouble—to learn what the Bible is, how its various parts are to be read and understood, why some parts are more meaningful and authoritative than others, and where its greatest treasures are to be found.

I can't promise that *all* your questions about the Bible will be answered in the pages that follow. I very much doubt that they will be. What I've tried to do is to plant warning flags on some of the chief stumbling blocks to

Bible reading and to point out ways around them; to set down the essential facts that you need to know about the contents of the Bible, the way they're arranged, the peculiar shorthand that's used to identify Biblical passages, and the various translations and editions in which the Bible appears; and to outline a reading plan that will enable you to cover the most important and rewarding sections of the Bible without "bogging down in the begats."

All kinds of readers are welcome except one. I don't want anyone beginning this book with the notion that he can read it *instead* of the actual Scriptures. My sole purpose is to introduce you to your Bible so that you can find out for yourself why it is known as "The Book of Life."

YOUR BIBLE

I

THE WORD OF GOD

Writing jacket blurbs for the Bible would be an adman's dream job. You could make the most startling statements—"Now in Its 100,000th Printing" . . . "Has Headed Best-Seller List for 400 Years"—and they would not be exaggerations. As for endorsements, your only problem would be deciding whom to quote:

"Best gift God ever gave to man"—Abraham Lincoln.

"Through its pages, as through a window divinely opened, all men can look into the stillness of eternity"—Thomas Carlyle.

"An invaluable and inexhaustible mine of knowledge and virtue"—John Quincy Adams.

"A book surpassing all others"—Napoleon.

"It finds me at greater depths of my being than any other book"—Samuel Taylor Coleridge.

"I find more sure marks of authenticity in the Bible than in any profane history whatever"—Sir Isaac Newton.

"A knowledge of the Bible without a college course is more valuable than a college course without a knowledge of the Bible"—William Lyon Phelps.

The Bible is worth reading simply as literature. If you know where to look, you will find in it some of the world's greatest poetry, as well as superb short stories, fables, epigrams, songs, dramatic monologues, letters, and biographies. One of the purposes of this book is to provide you with a guide to some of these literary treasures.

But if the Bible were merely good literature, you wouldn't find men like Lincoln using such unrestrained superlatives to express their appreciation of it. After all, there is other good literature.

What makes the Bible special is the conviction held by Lincoln and millions of others through the centuries that *God speaks to men through this book*.

It is crucial to understand just what is meant by that statement. Perhaps the greatest obstacle to Bible reading in our time is the confusion that has been created in the minds of laymen by two extreme views of the Bible.

TAKING IT LITERALLY

Biblical literalism is one of these extreme views. Contrary to popular impression, the literalist does not contend that every passage of the Bible must be "taken literally." He knows there are many metaphors and other figures of speech in the Scriptures. He will even acknowledge that the Bible contains fiction as well as fact: not even the most thoroughgoing literalist would deny that Jesus' parables were made-up stories designed to illustrate a point.

Literalism gets its name from its insistence that what we find in the Bible is not just the Word of God but the very *words* of God. The distinction is of tremendous importance. The phrase "Word of God," as used in the Bible itself, notably in the opening sentences of the Fourth Gospel, is an English translation of a Greek word, *Logos,* which was in wide use among philosophers at the time the New Testament was written. It connotes the creative, outgoing, self-revealing activity of God. The *Logos* was not a particular divine utterance, but God's overall message to mankind. It was not necessarily communicated verbally in speech or writing. Indeed, the whole point of Christianity is that the supreme communication of the Word took place when it was expressed through a human life and personality in Jesus Christ.

To the Biblical literalist, however, the Bible is the "Word of God" in the sense of containing a series of divine utterances. Some literalists depict God as dictating every sentence of the Bible to human scribes. Others, while rejecting that mechanical concept, assert that the human authors of the Scriptures were so firmly and explicitly guided by the Holy Spirit that what they wrote may be taken as having been spoken by God Himself. In other words, they insist that divine supervision of the writing of the Bible did not end with seeing that it included essential truths about God and man, but extended to the actual choice of words in which those truths were formulated.

There are two inescapable corollaries to the literalist view. One is that all parts of the Bible must be regarded as equal in authority. No greater historical credence may be attached to the account of the Resurrection than to the story of Jonah's being swallowed by a great fish. The Sermon on the Mount may be accorded no greater reverence as a guide to moral conduct than the Old Testament passage (2 Kings 2:24) which tells about an angry prophet summoning she-bears from the woods to gobble up some naughty children who had made fun of his bald head.

THERE ARE CONTRADICTIONS

The other conclusion which necessarily stems from the literalist view is that the Bible is totally free of error. If a statement is considered to have come directly from God, then it must be factually correct, no matter how sharply it may seem to conflict with scientific knowledge or common sense. To acknowledge even one small error of fact or historical detail in the Bible would, by the logic of Biblical literalism, discredit the whole book.*

The literalist view may be challenged, on purely empirical grounds, by pointing out that there are obviously many different levels of spirituality and wisdom in the Scriptures, just as there are obviously a number of factual errors and contradictions.

But there is a more serious objection to Biblical literalism on theological grounds. The whole idea of an infallible book is profoundly contrary to what the Bible itself tells us about God's way of revealing Himself to man. The Old Testament shows how God made Himself known, gradually and patiently over many centuries, by entering

* Some literalists have found a convenient loophole in the doctrine that only the *original manuscripts* of the Scriptures were totally free of error. This makes it possible to blame careless copyists for such manifest mistakes as the description of a vessel made for Solomon's temple which was "round, ten cubits from brim to brim . . . and a line of thirty cubits measured its circumference." As every schoolboy who has wrestled with *pi* can testify, the circumference would be 31.416 cubits.

into an intensely personal and often stormy relationship with a particular group of people, the Jews, whom He had chosen to be light-bearers to mankind. The prophets and kings and other leaders through whom God spoke remained very human and very fallible. Even the best of them—like the great King David—were guilty of sordid and selfish acts, which are plainly recorded in the Bible, as though to drive home the point that no matter how open they may have been to God's guidance they remained weak and imperfect human beings.

In the New Testament, it is spelled out even more plainly. The basic belief of Christianity—the lynchpin doctrine on which all else depends—is that God emptied Himself of His transcendental majesty and took on the limitations of humanity in the person of Jesus Christ. The Church has always taught that Jesus was *fully human* as well as fully divine, and early in its history it condemned as heresy a school of theology (called *Docetism*) which held that Jesus only seemed to be a man and was not really subject to human limitations. If you read the gospels with Jesus' true humanity in mind, you will discover many instances in which he was obviously weary, discouraged, and irritable. You will also see that he shared the medical opinion, universal among the people of his time, that insanity was caused by demons, and the equally prevalent geographical view that the earth was flat. If Jesus hadn't believed those things, he would not have been genuinely a man of his times. But the fact that he didn't know all that we now know (or think we know) about psychiatry and astronomy in no way impeaches the credibility of his teachings about the nature of God and the destiny of man. On those supremely important matters, he spoke with a unique authority.

To ascribe infallibility to the authors of the Bible is to

contend that God refused to accept in their case the risks
and limitations which He gladly assumed in the Incarnation. It is a form of Docetism which denies the humanity
of the Bible.

All heresies have consequences—that is why they are
dangerous. A Docetic view of the Scriptures leads all too
often to a tendency to put the Bible in Christ's rightful
place at the center of Christian devotion. Instead of putting his whole trust in the living Christ as the Way, the
Truth, and the Life, the man who boasts of believing the
Bible literally may feel that he can earn his own salvation
by unswerving faith in verbal propositions which can be
prefaced by the sacred formula, "the Bible says. . . ."

Martin Luther saw all this very clearly. That is why he
referred to the Bible as "the cradle wherein we find
Christ." It is a fatal error, he said, to bestow upon the
cradle the adoration which belongs to its occupant.

THE OTHER EXTREME

At the opposite extreme from literalism is the attitude
of *radical skepticism*. Whereas the literalist ignores the
human element in the Bible, the skeptic slights or denies
its divine element. He looks upon the Bible as an interesting compendium of ancient writings, and will go so far as
to acknowledge that some parts of it may be a reasonably
authentic record of events in which men felt that they
were confronted by God. But in deciding which passages
he will accept, he proceeds on the *a priori* assumption
that miracles can't happen. So he automatically writes off
any Biblical account of a wondrous happening which suggests that there is an order of reality transcending the ob-
servable regularities of nature and occasionally breaking
in upon them.

Nor is radical skepticism content with jettisoning the Bible's miracle stories. It also dismisses other passages on the grounds that they reflect the ignorance and prejudice of a particular age, or the propaganda interests of the Church at a certain stage of its development. Its basic rule of Biblical interpretation is: "When in doubt, throw it out." And the highest scores in the game of radical reductionism are awarded to pedagogues who find the most novel and far-fetched reasons for doubting that any part of the Bible really means what it says.

It is important to draw a clear distinction between radical skepticism and Biblical criticism. The former is an attitude, the latter is a tool. It is no reflection on a tool that it can be used foolishly and destructively as well as wisely and constructively. A hammer can be employed to drive nails or to bash heads. In the same way, the techniques of Biblical criticism can be used to make the Bible more meaningful, or to buttress the preconceptions of those who are prepared to believe almost anything about it except the fact that God had something to do with its production.

WHAT IS MEANT BY "BIBLICAL CRITICISM"

When we speak of Biblical criticism, we are using the word *criticism* not in the popular sense of derogatory judgment but rather in its original primary meaning of discriminating study. Since the early nineteenth century, scholars in Europe and America have made tremendous strides in discriminating study of the Bible. They have learned how to detect and correct textual errors by comparing a large number of old manuscripts. From very ancient documents found in caves around the Dead Sea and in the hot dry sands of Egypt, they have gained new insights into the Hebrew and Greek languages in which the Bible was written, and thus can make far more accurate translations. From archaeological digs and historical research, they have acquired a better understanding of places, events, cultures, and customs reflected in the Bible. (To give just one example out of hundreds, they now know that Abraham was not being cowardly or tricky, but was simply following the established protocol of his native Mesopotamia, when he introduced his wife as his sister.) Form criticism—the study of various literary forms used by authors of the Bible—has furnished clues to which sections can be read as literal history, and which are poems, parables, proverbs, and myths whose timeless truths are not dependent on whether the events described actually happened. *

Those who approach the Bible with an attitude of radical skepticism often find it convenient to bolster their preconceptions with glib references to "the assured results of modern criticism." The ploy is easy to master: If you want to discredit any portion of the Bible, you simply say, *"Of course,* modern criticism has shown that we can't put any stock in *that."*

This is hogwash. It is unfair to the scholars whose patient and objective investigations have cast so much helpful new light on the Bible. It also is an insult to the Bible.

* This is a good place to stress the point that Biblical scholars use the word "myth" in a special, technical sense which is quite different from the popular meaning of an untrue story. In Biblical parlance, a myth is a literary form which tells about other-worldly things in this-worldly concepts. To ask whether the events described in a myth "actually happened" is as pointless as wondering whether there really was a Prodigal Son, or a Good Samaritan. The only thing that matters about a myth is whether it succeeds in conveying an insight into some great truth about God or man which could not be adequately expressed in more pedestrian prose.

ARCHAEOLOGICAL EVIDENCE

The fact is that modern critical study, far from discrediting the Bible, has authenticated it to a far greater degree than most church members realize. When archaeologists dig into trackless desert wastes at a spot where the Bible says a city used to stand thousands of years ago, they find the ruins of houses and walls. (They have even found the remains of wells, precisely where the Old Testament says Jacob dug them.) When philologists examine the library of an Essene sect found in the Qumran caves near the Dead Sea, they find that the Fourth Gospel, once regarded as "too Greek" in its thought forms to have been written during the apostolic age, probably did come from the pen of a first-century Jew. When form critics seek to extract the biography of a simple human teacher from the story of Jesus, they find that the New Testament simply won't permit it. There is only one Christ in the gospels— the risen Christ whom the Church proclaims as Lord— and no amount of analysis will yield the simple human teacher that skepticism insists must be in there somewhere.

The overall results of modern criticism are well summarized in the words of William F. Albright of Johns Hopkins University, one of the world's greatest Biblical scholars and a leading figure in the critical movement: "There has been a general return to appreciation of the Bible's accuracy, both in general sweep and in factual detail. The substantial historicity of the Old and New Testaments has been vindicated to an extent I should have thought impossible forty years ago."

Although radical skepticism glibly employs the language of scholarship, it is in fact as intellectually indefensible as Biblical literalism. It is not an "open-minded" but a close-minded attitude. It *assumes* that the Creator of the universe will never under any circumstances intervene in its flow of events, and on the basis of that highly debatable hypothesis it would make liars of eyewitnesses who posted their lives as bond to their sincerity. Karl Barth, the "giant among pygmies" of twentieth-century theology, has said all that needs be said about the temerity, not to say arrogance, of this attitude:

"The post-Biblical theologian," says Barth, "may, no doubt, possess a better astronomy, geography, zoology, psychology, physiology, and so on, than these Biblical witnesses possessed. But he is not justified in comporting himself as though he knew more about the Word of God than they. . . . Still less is he authorized to look over their shoulder, to correct their reports, or to give them good, average or bad marks.

"Even the smallest, strangest, simplest or obscurest among the Biblical witnesses has an incomparable advantage over even the most pious, scholarly and sagacious latter-day theologian."

He was there.

THE MIDDLE ROAD

Fortunately, the Bible reader does not have to choose between the literalist approach which denies the humanity of the Bible or the skeptical approach which denies its divinity. There is still another view of the Bible, which does not require you to abandon either your intelligence or your faith. It might be called the ecumenical view, because it commands the support of many of the best Biblical scholars both in the Roman Catholic Church and in the mainstream Protestant denominations. It is consistent with the norms for Biblical interpretation laid down for Catholics by the Second Vatican Council in its Decree on Revelation and with the Statement on Scripture and Tradition adopted by the Consultation on Church Union as a basis for a merger of major U.S. Protestant denominations. It says in effect:

> The Bible is a book in which both God and man have had a hand. Its human authors retained all of the limitations of their humanity. This means that they inevitably made mistakes. They reflected the world-view of a pre-scientific age. They did not always understand clearly what God was trying to say to them and through them, with the result that they sometimes attributed to Him deeds, desires, and attitudes which we now know to be foreign to His true nature. But even in the most primitive passages of the Old Testaments, we can see God at work among His people, opening their eyes to new and deeper truth, and leading them toward the day when the Way, the Truth, and the Life would appear among them in person.

This view of the Bible attaches primary importance to the New Testament account of Jesus Christ, in whom God's self-disclosure reached its climax. It accepts the teaching and example of Christ as the ultimate yardstick by which all else in the Bible is to be measured. It affirms the historical authenticity of the gospels in all essential details, but allows room for the possibility of minor errors of fact which do not affect the basic story. It also acknowledges that some of the important parts of the story may be told through literary forms other than simple journalism. (For example, Matthew's account of the Sermon on the Mount may be a literary device for gathering together in one place teachings which Jesus gave at many different times.)

It reveres the Old Testament, even as Jesus did. But it expects to find there myth as well as history, fiction as well as fact, evil men as well as good ones, sordid stories as well as inspiring ones. It values all of these varied materials, not as the literal words of God, but as a record left by men who were caught up in the great events of history through which God made Himself known.

If you adopt this view of the Bible, you can read it critically—in the scholarly sense—without drifting into a confused skepticism. What is even more important, you can read it devotionally, without caring a great deal whether a particular passage happens to be an ancient folk story or a literal account of something that actually happened.

LISTEN TO WHAT GOD SAYS TO YOU

To read the Bible devotionally means to listen for what God is saying *to you* in its pages. This may sound like a lot of pious mumbo-jumbo. But it is the sober testimony of Christians of all ages, all cultures, and all branches of the Church—Protestant, Catholic, Anglican, and Orthodox—that God does speak to individual human hearts directly and personally through the Scriptures. And He does so in the most unpredictable ways. You can never tell what part of the Bible is going to come alive for you, and cast a sudden illumination over your problems. You may find your particular pearl of great price in a well-marked treasure-trove like the Sermon on the Mount, or it may pop out of a Psalm . . . or one of Paul's letters . . . or even from the dreary chronicle of the misdeeds of Israel's kings.

You well may wonder how the Eternal God can speak

to you, here and now, through the pages of a book written long ago. The answer is that God is always present within each of us. This indwelling Presence is what Christians call the Holy Spirit. It is the Holy Spirit's voice we hear when the Bible "speaks to our condition." Obviously, the Holy Spirit can—and does—use other books as a medium of communicating with us on the level of conscious thought. (I am even prepared to acknowledge that the Spirit may, on occasion, address someone through a television program.) But Christian experience testifies that the Bible is particularly and especially and uniquely "God's book"—the place where we are most likely to hear His Word for us.

There is no way I know to prove this to anyone who has not experienced it. I can only urge you to try it, and find out for yourself.

II

THE BEST WAY
TO READ YOUR BIBLE

The first step in Bible reading is to obtain a Bible you can read. That may sound as obvious as the famous old English recipe for rabbit stew which begins, "First, catch thy hare." But it is amazing how many people neglect this essential preparation.

WHICH BIBLE?

Having a Bible is by no means the same thing as having a Bible you can read. Unless you've previously made a serious stab at Bible reading, the chances are that the Bible gathering dust around your house is the King James Version, if you're a Protestant, or the Douay-Rheims Translation, if you're a Catholic.

These have been the most widely-used English translations of the Scriptures for three and a half centuries. They deserve veneration not only for their antiquity, but also for the tremendous role they have played in shaping the thoughts and lives of generations of Americans, Englishmen, Scotsmen, Canadians, Australians, and other English-speaking people. The King James Version particularly commands admiration for its literary style. Nowhere outside Shakespeare has our native tongue been employed with as much grace and felicity as in this translation, completed by forty-seven Church of England scholars in A.D. 1611.

But the King James also resembles Shakespeare's writing in another respect: it is full of words and phrases which baffle the modern reader. English is a living language, and in the past 350 years, it has undergone considerable change. Hundreds of words and phrases found in the King James Version have either fallen into disuse or have acquired different meanings. In some cases, our meaning for a word is exactly the opposite of the seventeenth-century usage.* With patience, fortitude, and a good pony, the modern reader can make sense of the King James. But there are enough problems in Bible reading without taking on one that's totally unnecessary. It's much smarter to buy a Bible that has been translated into your own tongue, which is contemporary English.

Modern translations have another important advan-

---

* For example, the King James uses "let" in the sense of "hinder," "prevent" to mean "precede," "comprehend" for "overcome," "communicate" for "share," "by and by" for "immediately."

tage. Because of the advances made by Biblical criticism and the discovery of manuscripts much older and more reliable than those used by seventeenth-century scholars, the newest translations are more accurate than any previously available.

MODERN TRANSLATIONS

There are several excellent modern translations to choose from.

Many people like the informal, idiomatic style of The New English Bible which was translated directly from the original Bible tongues (mainly Hebrew in the Old Testament and Greek in the New Testament) by a distinguished team of scholars from Oxford and Cambridge universities.

Equally informal and idiomatic is the translation prepared by the noted English clergyman, J. B. Phillips. His decisions on how to render a particular passage may not carry as much authority as those reached by a committee of experts, but the Phillips Translation has a consistency of style which is possible only when the whole job is done by one man.

The Anchor Bible is a massive project of Biblical scholarship undertaken in the United States under the aegis of William F. Albright, whose eminence as a Bible scholar was mentioned in the previous chapter. It comprises thirty-eight volumes, each by a different scholar. Each volume contains an introduction, notes, and comment as well as a new translation of some portion of the Scriptures. It is an ecumenical venture in Bible translation, in the sense that Protestants, Catholics, and Jews are represented among the thirty-eight well-known scholars associated in the project. But it cannot properly be described as a "common Bible" because each volume bears the imprimatur only of its individual translator and does not necessarily reflect an interfaith consensus.

The Confraternity Bible is the work of Catholic scholars, under the wing of the Confraternity of Christian Doctrine. It is the first officially sponsored Catholic translation into English from the original languages. (The Douay-Rheims was a translation into English of Jerome's fourth-century Latin translation, which is commonly known as the Vulgate.) It is as contemporary in its idiom as the New English Bible and its style has already become familiar to American Catholics because it is the source of the Scripture readings used in the new vernacular Mass.

The Amplified Bible was produced by conservative American Protestant scholars who hit upon the device of using parenthetical language to clarify the meaning of the original Hebrew or Greek phrase being translated. Sometimes the words in parentheses are alternative or optional translations, designed to convey the flavor of the original phrase more fully than any single English rendition could do. For example, the opening words of Genesis are given as follows:

"In the beginning God (prepared, formed, fashioned) and created the heavens and the earth."

In other cases, the words inserted parenthetically are designed to clarify a sentence which otherwise might be obscure to a modern reader. Thus, in the Twenty-third Psalm, we read: "Your rod (to protect) and your staff (to guide), they comfort me."

The most widely used modern translation is the Revised Standard Version (commonly known as "the RSV"), which resulted from fifteen years of joint labor by dozens of America's foremost Protestant scholars. The great merit of the RSV is that it preserves the sentence structures and, wherever possible, the precise language which made the King James Version a literary masterpiece. The RSV translators substituted contemporary English usage for archaic seventeenth-century words wherever necessary to make the original meaning clear. In some instances, they corrected textual or translation errors. The result is just what the name "Revised Standard Version" implies—the King James in modern dress.

The highest tribute that has been paid to the accuracy of the RSV translation is its acceptance by Catholic authorities. In 1966, Richard Cardinal Cushing, Archbishop of Boston, gave his imprimatur to an RSV Bible for use by Catholics everywhere.

The RSV is available in a vast variety of editions, sizes, shapes, and prices. I would particularly commend to your attention The Oxford Annotated Bible. It contains excellent introductions to each book of the Bible, and many helpful footnotes which clarify obscure passages. It also contains full-color maps, extensive cross-references and other aids to study. The typography and layout are superb. One of the best things about this Bible is that you can buy it with or without the Apocrypha. (Never mind for the moment if you don't know what the Apocrypha is; we're coming to that shortly.) The Oxford Annotated Bible was edited by two of the world's most distinguished Biblical scholars, Herbert G. May of Oberlin College and Bruce M. Metzger of Yale Divinity School. Walter M. Abbott, a leading Catholic scholar, has called it "the best one-volume Bible on the market" and I am glad to append my humble amen to this judgment.

"THE LITTLE BOOKS"

Once you have acquired a readable Bible, the next step is to get acquainted with it. Riffle through the pages and you'll see that this is a most unusual kind of book. As a matter of precise fact, it is not *a* book at all. Our English word *Bible* is derived from the Greek *biblia*, which means "little books." The Bible is really a library of little books, written by different people, for different purposes, at different times stretching over a period of more than 1300 years. The earliest portions of the Old Testament date from before 1200 B.C. The latest parts of the New Testament were written after A.D. 100.

The Old Testament does not contain all of the Hebrew literature that was written before the time of Jesus nor does the New Testament contain all of the writings that circulated in the early Christian Church. In both cases, the library which we call the Bible represents a selection of a relatively few "little books" out of a great many that conceivably might have been included. The selection process was not carried out in what we would regard today as a neat, systematic fashion. No one conducted a poll, or summoned a convention to decide what should go in and what should be left out. The decision was simply a consensus which emerged gradually over a period of centuries.

THE SEPTUAGINT AND THE HEBREW CANON

The books chosen for inclusion in the Old Testament—what scholars call "the Old Testament canon"—were those which were held in the highest esteem within the Jewish community as faithful records of the physical and spiritual odyssey of the children of Israel. It is not surprising, therefore, to find that there are two different versions of the Old Testament canon. One was made some time during the period between 250 and 100 B.C., by a group of Jewish scholars living in Alexandria, Egypt, the queen city of the ancient Middle Eastern world. They translated the Hebrew scriptures into Greek, which was rapidly becoming the international language of the time. Their translation is known as *the Septuagint*. It was the Old Testament of the early Christian Church and was the version known and quoted by Jesus, as well as by St. Paul and other New Testament writers.

The other version of the Old Testament emerged in Jerusalem some time prior to A.D. 100, and is known as *the Hebrew canon.*

The only basic difference between the Septuagint and the Hebrew canon is that the former contains several books which are not found in the latter. These writings have come to be called the *Apocrypha.* They found their way into the Latin Vulgate, which was based on the Septuagint, and hence into all Catholic Bibles until this day. Protestant editions of the Bible usually follow the Hebrew canon and omit the Aprocryphal books. The Anglican Communion, which includes the Episcopal Church in the United States, takes the middle view that the Apocryphal writings are good and useful books, which should be read, but which are not to be used to establish any point of doctrine. The translators of the King James and Revised Standard versions evidently shared this viewpoint: they included the Apocryphal writings but segregated them from the rest of the Old Testament. In recent years, Protestants have taken a growing interest in the Apocrypha, and most Biblical scholars think this is a healthy trend.

Here are the thirty-nine books of the Old Testament which are included in the Hebrew canon, in the order in which they appear in the RSV Bible:

> Genesis
> Exodus
> Leviticus
> Numbers
> Deuteronomy
> Joshua
> Judges
> Ruth
> The First Book of Samuel
> The Second Book of Samuel
> The First Book of Kings
> The Second Book of Kings
> The First Book of Chronicles
> The Second Book of Chronicles
> Ezra
> Nehemiah
> Esther
> Job
> Psalms
> Proverbs
> Ecclesiastes
> Song of Solomon
> Isaiah
> Jeremiah
> Lamentations
> Ezekiel
> Daniel
> Hosea
> Joel
> Amos

Obadiah
Jonah
Micah
Nahum
Habakkuk
Zephaniah
Haggai
Zechariah
Malachi

Here are the fifteen books or portions of books which are included in the RSV translation of the Apocrypha:

The First Book of Esdras
The Second Book of Esdras
Tobit
Judith
Additions to the Old Testament Book of Esther
Wisdom of Solomon
Ecclesiasticus
Baruch
The Letter of Jeremiah
The Prayer of Azariah
Susanna
Bel and the Dragon
The Prayer of Manasseh
The First Book of the Maccabees
The Second Book of the Maccabees

The New Testament canon includes twenty-seven "little books" which the early Christian churches adjudged to be the most authentic and helpful of the numerous writings which circulated during the apostolic and post-apostolic era.

THE GOSPELS AND THE
NEW TESTAMENT CANON

The four gospels which are the heart of the New Testament were selected for transmission to posterity over many other attempts to record the life and teachings of Jesus. Many of the writings which the early Church passed over have disappeared, but some have recently come to light again after all these centuries. One of the most exciting archaeological discoveries of modern times was a collection of documents which turned up at Nag Hammadi in Egypt at about the same time that the Dead Sea Scrolls were recovered in Palestine. Among the Nag Hammadi scrolls was a copy of the long-lost "Gospel of Thomas" which scholars had previously known about only through references in the writings of some of the early Church fathers. "Thomas" is interesting primarily as a vindication of the good judgment exercised by the early Church in deciding which writings should be preserved. It contains a number of teachings of Jesus which parallel sayings long familiar from the New Testament gospels, plus other material which bears the unmistakable stamp of the Gnostic heresies which sprang up in some parts of the Church during the second century A.D.*

Although it was not until the fourth century that the canon of the New Testament was finally and officially fixed, the Church had reached a consensus long before that on the authoritative status to be accorded to the gospels of Matthew, Mark, Luke, and John, the Book of Acts, and the letters of Paul. Most of the argument was over

* Gnosticism is a complicated business, and we can't go into all of the intricacies of its doctrines here. You'll find it discussed at length in any good book of early Church history. Basically, the Gnostics thought that inside information (Greek *gnosis* or knowledge) was the key to salvation.

the Letter of James and the Book of Revelation. It might be noted that although these writings were ultimately given a place in the New Testament, they were destined to remain bones of contention. Twelve centuries later, Martin Luther scornfully dismissed James as "an epistle of straw." And Revelation is *still* so troublesome that many Protestants act as if it weren't in the Bible.

Here are the twenty-seven books of the New Testament recognized by all branches of the Christian Church:

The Gospel According to Matthew
The Gospel According to Mark
The Gospel According to Luke
The Gospel According to John
The Book of the Acts of the Apostles
The Letter of Paul to the Romans
The First Letter of Paul to the Corinthians
The Second Letter of Paul to the Corinthians
The Letter of Paul to the Galatians
The Letter of Paul to the Ephesians
The Letter of Paul to the Philippians
The Letter of Paul to the Colossians
The First Letter of Paul to the Thessalonians
The Second Letter of Paul to the Thessalonians
The First Letter of Paul to Timothy
The Second Letter of Paul to Timothy
The Letter of Paul to Titus
The Letter of Paul to Philemon
The Letter to the Hebrews
The Letter of James
The First Letter of Peter
The Second Letter of Peter
The First Letter of John
The Second Letter of John

The Third Letter of John
The Letter of Jude
The Book of Revelation

It's not necessary to memorize the foregoing lists. But
you may find it helpful to read them two or three times to
fix in your mind the approximate order of the Bible's
books. If you know that Exodus is near the front, Paul's
letters near the back, and the Psalms close to the middle
of the Bible, you will save yourself a lot of fumbling
around when you're looking for something.

CHAPTER AND VERSE

Biblical books are divided into *chapters,* which are usually much shorter than the chapters of a modern book.
Each chapter is further divided into numbered *verses.*
This format was an invention of mediaeval printers. (The
original manuscripts run everything together in a dense
mass of words.) Some modern Bibles de-emphasize the
chapter-and-verse system in favor of contemporary para-
graphing, but they continue to indicate the chapter-and-
verse numbers in the margins.

As you probably know, it is customary to cite a particular passage of Scripture by giving book, chapter, and verse
or verses in that order. Exodus 20:3 refers to the Book of
Exodus, chapter 20, verse 3. Exodus 20:3–11 would mean
the third through the eleventh verses of chapter 20.

But suppose you don't know the chapter and verse?
How do you track down something which you vaguely remember as being "somewhere in the Bible"?

HOW TO USE A CONCORDANCE

You look it up in a concordance. A concordance is a
special kind of index, which enables you to find any verse

of Scripture of which you can recall one or two key words. You simply look in the concordance, under the key word you recall, and you will find listed all of the verses of the Bible in which that word appears. You don't have to know the first word of the verse: any key noun or verb will do.

For example, you may recall having once heard a verse of Scripture that deals harshly with busybodies. Look under *busybodies* in any standard concordance, and you'll find that the verse you're looking for is "2 Thess. 3:11." So you turn to Paul's second letter to the Thessalonians, and in chapter 3, verse 11, you'll read: "For we hear that some of you are living in idleness, mere busybodies, not doing any work."

Or you can use a concordance to find a familiar Biblical story, simply by remembering one of the distinctive words that appear in the story. Take the story of the birth of Moses, for example. Where did his mother hide the baby? In the *bulrushes*, of course. So you look up bulrushes, and the concordance sends you to the second chapter of Exodus.

THE MOST IMPORTANT PASSAGES

To spare you the necessity of consulting a concordance during the period when you're getting acquainted with your Bible, here is a where-to-find-it guide to a few of the more important and/or familiar passages of Scripture:

The Nativity story	Luke 2:1–21
The preparatory ministry of John the Baptist	Luke 3:1–20
Jesus' temptation in the wilderness	Luke 4:1–13
Jesus begins his ministry	Mark 1:14–45
The Sermon on the Mount	Matthew 5–7

The saga of Abraham, Isaac, and Jacob	Genesis 11:27–37:1
The story of Joseph and his brothers	Genesis 37:2–50:26
Moses leads the children of Israel out of Egypt	Exodus 1:8–15:21
How Joshua fought the battle of Jericho	Joshua 6:1–21
Gideon routs an army with 300 picked men	Judges 7:1–23
The story of Samson and Delilah	Judges 13:2–17:31
God calls Samuel to lead Israel	1 Samuel 1:1–28; 3:1–20
Israel's first king: the story of Saul	1 Samuel 8:4–31:13
David and Goliath	1 Samuel 17:1–54
The reign of King David: Israel's golden age	2 Samuel 1:1 to 1 Kings 2:11
King Solomon's wisdom, wealth, and wives	1 Kings 3:1–4:34; 10:1–11:43
The building of the temple in Jerusalem	1 Kings 5:1–8:66
Isaiah's vision	Isaiah 6:1–13
Isaiah's prophecy of the Messiah	Isaiah 9:2–7; 11:1–9
Shadrach, Meshach, and Abednego	Daniel 3
Daniel in the lion's den	Daniel 6
God's judgment on social injustice	Amos 5:6–24
The story of Jonah and the great fish	Jonah 1:1–2:10

READ A FEW MINUTES EVERY DAY

The Bible contains more than 500,000 words of prose and poetry. Even if it were as easy to read as an historical novel (and some parts of it are), it could not be devoured at a few sittings. Reading the Bible is a long-term project, and should be pursued at a leisurely pace.

The best approach is to spend a few minutes with the Bible every day. Put your Bible in a convenient place— beside your bed or easy chair—where you'll be sure to see it daily. If possible, set aside a regular time for Bible reading—first thing in the morning, last thing at night, or whenever you find most suitable.

How much you read on any given day will depend, of course, on your own preferences. But I think you will find it more satisfactory not to set an arbitrary quota. Reading the Bible is rather like working a gold mine. The lode is rich in some spots, thin in others. In the New Testament and in some parts of the Old Testament, you can count on turning up nuggets with virtually every bite of the shovel. But there are stretches of the Old Testament in which you'll have to dig through quite a lot of ore to find a few flecks of gold dust.

As a rough rule of thumb, I recommend that you begin by reading a chapter a day in the New Testament. This will be enough to provide you with abundant material for thought and reflection during the next twenty-four hours.

If you wish to read more than one chapter a day, there is no law against it. But, to switch the metaphor from gold to gastronomy, remember that the Bible is rich food. To digest it properly you should take small bites and chew them thoroughly.

The chapter-a-day rule can also be applied to the meatier portions of the Old Testament, such as Genesis, Exodus, Job, the Psalms, Isaiah, Amos, and Jeremiah. You can increase your stint to several chapters a day without strain when you come to smooth-flowing narratives such as the stories of Ruth and Esther, or love poetry such as the Song of Solomon, or true adventures such as the history of King David. And there are some sections of the Old Testament, such as the dreary accounts of Israel's minor kings and their perpetual wars in the two books of Chronicles, which you can skim through very rapidly, or skip altogether, without grievous loss. (You'll find more detailed advice on this in the Old Testament reading plan outlined in subsequent chapters.)

THE BAFFLING PASSAGES

The oldest parts of the Bible were written more than 3000 years ago. The newest parts are nearly 2000 years old. In any literature of great antiquity—whether it be Homer's poetry, Sophocles' plays, or the Bible—you can expect to encounter allusions to persons and places, as well as figures of speech, which are meaningless to you. Modern translations may minimize this difficulty, but they cannot eliminate it entirely without becoming rewrites rather than translations. Reference Bibles, such as the Oxford Annotated Bible mentioned earlier, contain footnotes which will clear up many of the remaining mysteries. You will also find it helpful to study maps of the Bible lands in order to get a clear picture of the geography relevant to the story. Most reference Bibles contain such maps. There also are Bible atlases, if you are the kind who really goes for visual aids.

Occasionally, you will come to a passage which baffles you in spite of all the guidance you can obtain from footnotes or maps. If it's a minor matter, you may prefer to pass on to something else. It is not really necessary that you understand every obscure verse in the Bible. But if your curiosity is aroused to the point where you're willing to do a little research, scholars have written whole libraries of reference books illuminating the historical, economic, political, cultural, linguistic, and religious background of virtually every sentence in the Bible.

These encyclopedic reference books are called *commentaries*. One of the most comprehensive is The Interpreter's Bible. I can't advise you to buy one for home use, since it runs to twelve large, expensive volumes. But you can find it in most libraries. If you become a serious student of the Bible and want a reference book ready at hand, there are several good one-volume commentaries on the market. I particularly recommend The Abingdon Bible Commentary, which is about the size of an unabridged dictionary, and quite modestly priced.

I mention these resources because I believe that you'll get the most out of the Bible if you are prepared not merely to read it but to study it. But don't be scared off by all this talk about footnotes, maps, and commentaries. You will find that a very large portion of the Bible's treasure is lying right out in the open. Even if all of the difficult passages were excised from the Bible, there would remain, in plain, unmistakable language, as much truth as any man needs to live by.

THE ONE INDISPENSABLE REQUIREMENT

The one indispensable requirement is that you read the Bible attentively. You are not reading this book for its entertainment value (although it is surprisingly rich in that). Nor are you primarily in search of information about things that happened long ago and far away. You are seeking light for *your* pathway, here and now. And you will find it, if you give the Bible a chance—or, to put it more accurately, if you give God a chance to speak to you through the Bible.

This does not mean that you can expect to find in every chapter a sort of special-delivery letter from God telling you exactly how to cope with your immediate problems. Relatively little of the Bible is taken up with didactic advice, moral commandments, exhortations, and that sort of thing. Like a good novel, the Bible makes most of its important points indirectly. The characters are not so much described as they are depicted in action. And that includes the principal character—God. We find God dealing with men—all sorts and conditions of men—over a long period of time and in a vast variety of situations. From the whole Biblical record there emerges a picture of God and His attitude toward men which, however inadequate and partial it may be, is far more enlightening than any we might construct from philosophical speculation or an abstract recital of theological dogma.

The Bible's story of God-in-action reaches its climax in the New Testament gospels, where we see, in the life of Jesus Christ, as much of the divine nature as can be expressed in human terms. And even here, the Biblical writers are usually content to let the story speak for itself. They tell us what Jesus did and said on specific occasions, and let us draw our own conclusions about the kind of person he was. It is a remarkable fact that not one of the gospels contains a physical description of Jesus.

So we read the Bible to find out what God is like. We also learn a great deal—more than most of us find comfortable—about what *we* are like. There is no other work of literature, not even Shakespeare at his best, which rivals the Bible for realistic, penetrating insights into human nature. In its pages we are confronted with all the glory and the grubbiness, the courage and the cowardice, the wisdom and the folly, the nobility and the wickedness of which men are capable. In its "cast of thousands" the Bible includes magnificent heroes, memorable heels—and characters like David who are part hero and part heel.

IDENTIFY WITH THE CHARACTERS

To read the Bible attentively means to identify with its human characters whenever you can see yourself in them —in other words, become involved in the story as a participant rather than a spectator. To do this requires both honesty and common sense. On the one hand, you must be aware of the ubiquitous power of human pride, which causes all of us to think ourselves better than we really are. On the other hand, you should not cultivate a guilty conscience when none is warranted. However great your shortcomings, you cannot possibly resemble *all* the sinners found in the Bible. If the shoe doesn't fit, don't force it onto your foot. Just try it on for size.

It is never easy for any of us to bring ourselves under the judgment of the Bible. The constant temptation is to reverse the relationship, and sit in judgment over the Bible. If we recognize that there are human elements in the Bible, we can twist this fact into a convenient alibi for ignoring any passage which contradicts our own ideas about right and wrong. This is what many Biblical literalists are afraid of, and their fear is by no means unfounded. But the answer does not lie in clinging desperately to a Docetic view of Biblical inspiration. The answer is to approach the Bible in the spirit of Christ—that is, humbly and openly, not seeking to justify ourselves, but attentively listening to what God has to say to us.

The person who comes to the Bible in this spirit will not find it necessary to worry about such questions as whether a great fish really swallowed Jonah, or exactly what kind of astronomical manifestation could have led the Wise

Men to believe that a star was located directly over a particular stable in Bethlehem.

It does not greatly matter whether the story of Jonah is actual history or an ancient legend. The *point* of the story is that God's love and forgiveness is extended not only to the children of Israel (or, in modern terms, to church members) but to all men. That was a tremendously important message to the Israelites of Jonah's day—and it is not altogether irrelevant to twentieth-century Christians.

Similarly, the point of Matthew's poetic account of the Wise Men's visit is that Christ's mission was universal, embracing Gentiles as well as Jews. (It would be equally true, and more pertinent today, to put it the other way around.)

THE BIBLE AS HISTORY

I do not mean to suggest that we can be indifferent to all questions of historicity. There are events—for example, the Exodus from Egypt in the Old Testament, and the Resurrection of Christ in the New Testament—which cannot be regarded as myths (however convenient that interpretation might be for doctrinaire disbelievers in miracles) without completely undermining the authority of the Bible. The Exodus and the Resurrection were crucial episodes in the formation of the Israelite nation and the Christian Church and the Bible presents them, plainly and unmistakably, as real historical events. If they did not actually take place, the whole Biblical story is based on fraud, and there is no good reason why we should continue reading it. Personally, I am satisfied that they *did* take place, and I have yet to encounter any persuasive evidence to the contrary.

An entire discipline called *hermeneutics* has developed around the question of how the various parts of the Bible are to be understood and interpreted. Any time you're really curious what the scholars think about a particular passage, you can consult a commentary (where you will most likely discover that several different opinions have been eloquently expounded). But there is a simple rule of thumb you can follow, if you prefer. I do not think it will ever lead you far astray. It is this:

If factuality is essential to the significance of an episode related in the Bible, it may be regarded as authentic history.

THE PARABLES

If we bear in mind that spiritual truth can be conveyed through parables, poems, novels, short stories, and other forms of fiction as well as through factual history and biography, we will minimize the number of occasions on which we find ourselves asking of a Biblical passage: "Did this really happen?" And that will free our minds for the important question: "What is God saying to *me* in this story?"

Don't be surprised if you ask the question without getting an immediate answer. This will happen most of the time. God does not use the Bible like a Ouija board. To hear what He has to say to you through its pages, you must be prepared to keep on listening patiently, and in the words of the Book of Common Prayer, to "read, mark, learn, and inwardly digest" much that does not seem particularly relevant to your needs at the moment.

"We are frequently advised to read the Bible with our own personal needs in mind, and to look for answers to our private questions," says Frederick C. Grant, one of

America's leading Bible scholars. "This is good as far as it goes. . . .

"But better still is the advice to study the Bible objectively . . . without regard, first of all, to our own subjective needs.

"Let the great passages fix themselves in our memory. Let them stay there permanently like bright beacons, launching their powerful shafts of light upon life's problems—our own and everyone's—as they illumine now one, now another dark area of human life.

"Following such a method, we discover that the Bible does 'speak to our condition' and meet our needs, not just occasionally, or when some emergency arises, but continually."

Palestine in the Days of Christ

III

A NEW TESTAMENT READING PLAN

If the Bible were a history book which embodied a continuous narrative, it would make sense to begin reading in the part which we encounter first when we open it—that is, in the Old Testament book of Genesis. But we have already noted that the Bible is properly regarded not as one book, but as a whole library of books. And if you went into a library to begin reading up on a topic, you would not necessarily begin with the first book you found on the shelf. Instead, you would seek the latest and most definitive treatment of the subject.

We read the Bible to learn what God is like, how He feels toward us, and what He expects of us. So it is best to begin with the part which tells about Jesus Christ, for in him we find the clearest answer ever offered man. I hope that you'll eventually read all the Bible. But if you suspect that you may bog down part way through the project, it is doubly important that you start with the New Testament.

Even in the New Testament, it's neither necessary nor desirable to "begin at the beginning." The remainder of this chapter will be devoted to outlining a New Testament reading plan which I think you'll find far more rewarding than the usual procedure of starting with Matthew's gospel and plowing straight through to the Book of Revelation.

I hope you'll use this chapter (and the chapters that will follow on the Old Testament and the Apocrypha) as a sort of treasure map of the Bible. Its purpose is to guide you past some of the bogs and morasses, and to make sure you don't overlook places where it's especially profitable to dig.

A map is most useful if you consult it as you move along. You could memorize it before you set out, and never look at it again. But it will work a lot better if you study each part of the route just before you actually traverse it. So I urge you to follow this procedure:

First, read the comments made herein about a particular segment of the Bible.

Then, go read that part of the Bible.

If you do your Bible reading on a chapter-a-day basis, several days, a week, or a month may go by before you are ready to return to this book for a briefing on the next step. The simplest solution is to keep this book with your Bible, just as you keep a road map in your car.

So much for the preliminaries. Now let's get on with the treasure hunt.

THE GOSPEL ACCORDING TO LUKE

I suggest that you begin with the GOSPEL ACCORD-ING TO LUKE. It is a relatively brief book, about 20,000 words, but it is universally recognized as a literary masterpiece. Many discriminating readers are prepared to go even further and say, with the nineteenth-century French historian Ernest Renan, that it is "the most beautiful book ever written."

The author does not identify himself by name, but most scholars accept the tradition of the early Church that this best of all gospels was written by Luke, the "beloved physician" who accompanied Paul on some of his missionary travels, including his final journey to Rome. From the few clues he provides in his writings, and from remarks about him in Paul's letters, it can be deduced that he was a Greek doctor whom Paul met in Antioch. If this deduction is valid, it means that Luke is the only Gentile author in the Bible.

Although Luke was a literary craftsman worthy of comparison with Shakespeare and Dante, he was first of all a reporter. His purpose, as he explained in a preface, was to "compile an account of the things which have been accomplished among us, just as they were delivered to us by those who from the beginning were eyewitnesses. . . ."

It is impossible to tell, at this great remove in time, exactly when Luke wrote his gospel. Some authorities put the date as early as A.D. 60, others as late as 90, with the majority favoring the decade 70–80. The exact date in any case is unimportant. What matters is that Luke gathered his material from men and women who had known

Jesus in the flesh, and who had seen firsthand the events which he describes. It is probable that Luke did much of his research during the two-year period (A.D. 57–59) he spent in Palestine waiting for his imprisoned friend Paul to be shipped to Rome for trial. It is obvious that Luke did a great deal of what reporters call legwork, interviewing scores if not hundreds of eyewitnesses. He also made use of written records which he considered reliable, including the previously circulated Gospel of Mark. One of Luke's sources, almost certainly, was the Virgin Mary. His story of the Nativity, which alone would be enough to insure him a place among the greatest writers in history, is written entirely from Mary's viewpoint.*

Much of what Luke reports about the life and ministry of Jesus is also found in one or more of the other gospels. But posterity is indebted to Luke alone for many magnificent little anecdotes which illuminate Jesus' character and personality. Only Luke, for example, tells us about Zacchaeus, the little short fellow who had to climb a sycamore tree in order to see over the throngs of people around Jesus. Jesus spotted him and, in a gesture full of warmth and humor, called the little man down from the tree to be his host at dinner.

THE TWO GREAT PARABLES

Luke also is exclusive with two great parables which convey the essence of Jesus' teachings so unforgettably that they can rightly be called "the Gospel in miniature." These are the parables of the Good Samaritan (Luke 10: 25–37), and of the Prodigal Son (Luke 15:11–32).

* The other account of the Nativity in the New Testament—found in Matthew's gospel—is told from Joseph's viewpoint.

Here is the story of the Good Samaritan as Luke tells it:

And behold, a lawyer stood up to put him to the test, saying, "Teacher, what shall I do to inherit eternal life?" He said to him, "What is written in the law? How do you read?" And he answered, "You shall love the Lord your God with all your heart, and with all your soul, and with all your strength, and with all your mind; and your neighbor as yourself." And he said to him, "You have answered right; do this, and you will live."

But he, desiring to justify himself, said to Jesus, "And who is my neighbor?" Jesus replied, "A man was going down from Jerusalem to Jericho, and he fell among robbers, who stripped him and beat him, and departed, leaving him half-dead. Now by chance a priest was going down that road; and when he saw him he passed by on the other side. So likewise a Levite, when he came to the place and saw him, passed by on the other side. But a Samaritan, as he journeyed, came to where he was; and when he saw him, he had compassion, and went to him and bound up his wounds, pouring on oil and wine; then he set him on his own beast and brought him to an inn, and took care of him. And the next day he took out two denarii and gave them to the innkeeper, saying, 'Take care of him; and whatever more you spend, I will repay you when I come back.' Which of these three do you think, proved neighbor to the man who fell among the robbers?" He said, "The one who showed mercy on him." And Jesus said to him, "Go and do likewise."

Luke 10:25–37

The story of the Prodigal Son is regarded by some discerning critics as the most perfect short story ever written:

And he said, "There was a man who had two sons; and the younger of them said to his father, 'Father, give me the share of property that falls to me.' And he divided his living between them. Not many days later, the younger son gathered all he had and took his journey into a far country, and there he squandered his property in loose living. And when he had spent everything, a great famine arose in that country, and he began to be in want. So he went and joined himself to one of the citizens of that country, who sent him into his fields to feed swine. And he would gladly have fed on the pods that the swine ate; and no one gave him anything. But when he came to himself he said, 'How many of my father's hired servants have bread enough and to spare, but I perish here with hunger! I will arise and go to my father, and I will say to him, "Father, I have sinned against heaven and before you; I am no longer worthy to be called your son; treat me as one of your hired servants."' And he arose and came to his father. But while he was yet at a distance, his father saw him and had compassion, and ran and embraced him and kissed him. And the son said to him, 'Father, I have sinned against heaven and before you; I am no longer worthy to be called your son.' But the father said to his servants, 'Bring quickly the best robe, and put it on him; and put a ring on his hand, and shoes on his feet; and bring the fatted calf and kill it, and let us eat and make merry; for this my son was dead, and is alive again; he was lost, and is found.' And they began to make merry.

"Now his elder son was in the field; and as he came and drew near to the house, he heard music and dancing. And he called one of the servants and asked what this meant. And he said to him, 'Your brother has come, and your father has killed the fatted calf, because he has received him safe and sound.' But he was angry and refused to go in. His father came out and entreated him, but he answered his father, 'Lo, these many years I have served you, and I never disobeyed your command; yet you never gave me a kid, that I might make merry with my friends. But when this son of yours came, who has devoured your living with harlots, you killed for him the fatted calf!' And he said to him, 'Son, you are always with me, and all that is mine is yours. It was fitting to make merry and be glad, for this your brother was dead, and is alive; he was lost, and is found.'"

Luke 15:11–32

Jesus' compassion for the poor and sick and oppressed, his unfailing understanding of all sorts and conditions of men, are so vividly portrayed by Luke that his is sometimes called "the gospel of mercy."

But you will also encounter in Luke the Jesus who sternly rebukes the complacent rich, the self-righteous, and the conventionally pious, and who bluntly warns, "If any man would come after me, let him take up his cross daily, and follow me."

There are several other things to watch for while you're reading Luke. One is his attitude toward women. He treats them as human beings—a rarity in his day—and gives them far more space than any other gospel writer. His poetry is also worthy of special note. The initial chapters contain three songs of such great beauty they have been used continuously for 1900 years in Christian liturgies. They are known, from their opening words in Latin, as the Magnificat, the Benedictus, and the Nunc Dimittis.

The Magnificat is Mary's song of exultation after she has been told that she will bear the Son of God:

> My soul magnifies the Lord,
> and my spirit rejoices in God my Savior,
> for he has regarded the low estate of his handmaiden.
> For behold, henceforth all generations will call me blessed;
> for he who is mighty has done great things for me,
> and holy is his name.
> And his mercy is on those who fear him
> from generation to generation.
> He has shown strength with his arm,
> he has scattered the proud in the imagination of their hearts,
> he has put down the mighty from their thrones,
> and exalted those of low degree;
> he has filled the hungry with good things,
> and the rich he has sent empty away.
> He has helped his servant Israel,
> in remembrance of his mercy,
> as he spoke to our fathers,
> to Abraham and to his posterity for ever.
>
> Luke 1:46–55

The Benedictus is the hymn of praise in which Zechariah, father of John the Baptist, anticipates the deliverance to be wrought by Christ:

> Blessed be the Lord God of Israel,
> for he has visited and redeemed his people,
> and has raised up a horn of salvation for us
> in the house of his servant David,

as he spoke by the mouth of his holy prophets from of
   old,
that we should be saved from our enemies,
and from the hand of all who hate us;
to perform the mercy promised to our fathers,
and to remember his holy covenant,
the oath which he swore to our father Abraham, to grant
   us
that we, being delivered from the hand of our enemies,
might serve him without fear,
in holiness and righteousness before him all the days of
   our life.
And you, child, will be called the prophet of the Most
   High;
for you will go before the Lord to prepare his ways,
to give knowledge of salvation to his people
in the forgiveness of their sins,
through the tender mercy of our God,
when the day shall dawn upon us from on high
to give light to those who sit in darkness
   and in the shadow of death,
to guide our feet into the way of peace.

                                              Luke 1:68–79

The Nunc Dimittis is the prayer uttered by a devout
old Jew named Simeon after he saw the child Jesus:

Lord, now lettest thou thy servant depart in peace,
according to thy word;
for mine eyes have seen thy salvation
which thou hast prepared in the presence of all peoples,
a light for revelation to the Gentiles,
and for glory to thy people Israel.

                                              Luke 2:29–32

Luke's gospel does have some shortcomings, to be sure. He gives us only a fraction of the Sermon on the Mount recorded by Matthew. And his truncated version of the Lord's Prayer is far less satisfactory than Matthew's. His theological concepts are less profound than those found in the Gospel according to John and in Paul's letters. The early Church knew what it was doing when it preserved other writings as well as Luke's gospel. But if you were going to read only one book of the Bible, most Biblical scholars would recommend that it be Luke.

ACTS

THE ACTS OF THE APOSTLES is a sequel to the Gospel of Luke, by the same author. Picking up where the gospel leaves off, it describes Jesus' departure from his disciples, and the "Great Commission" which he gave them to preach the good news to all men everywhere. The remainder of the book tells how the mission was carried out over the next three decades, until the Apostle Paul reached Rome in about A.D. 62.

Acts is invaluable as a history of the crucial formative years of the Church. Although it is an intensely human book, its real hero is the Holy Spirit, whose dramatic impact on the apostles is described in the second chapter of Acts. This account of the first day of Pentecost is one of the finest examples of Luke's literary skill. "Nowhere in the Bible," says Mary Ellen Chase in her fine book *The Bible and the Common Reader*, "is better narrative than this." Contemporary readers may be puzzled by some of the phenomena, such as "speaking in tongues," which Luke describes.* But there is no mistaking the reality of the

---

* In recent years, there has been a revival of interest in glossolalia or tongue-speaking in some of the mainline Protestant bodies, such as the Episcopal Church, as well as in the so-called Pentecostal sects.

apostles' experience, or their sense of having suddenly been filled with a power and a wisdom not their own:

> When the day of Pentecost had come, they were all together in one place. And suddenly a sound came from heaven like the rush of a mighty wind, and it filled all the house where they were sitting. And there appeared to them tongues as of fire, distributed and resting on each one of them. And they were all filled with the Holy Spirit and began to speak in other tongues, as the Spirit gave them utterance.
>
> Now there were dwelling in Jerusalem Jews, devout men from every nation under heaven. And at this sound the multitude came together, and they were bewildered, because each one heard them speaking in his own language.
>
> Acts 2:1–6

In Acts, as in the gospel which bears his name, Luke proves himself a diligent and careful reporter. The first half of the book is evidently based on material he gathered from interviews with people like Peter and Paul, and from documents circulated in the early Church. But in the later chapters, when he is relating the harrowing details of Paul's missionary journeys, shipwrecks, arrests, and other adventures, the pronoun "we" appears in the narrative. Luke is now doing what every reporter likes best—telling about things he saw with his own eyes. And he does it superbly.

A fellow writer is impressed by the fact that Luke is invariably specific about people (he mentions no less than 110 individuals by name), places, times, and events. He has a great sense of local color, and tells you not only what Paul said in his sermons, but how they traveled, where they lodged, by whom they were entertained, etc.

Biblical scholars have cross-checked every statement Luke makes against historical and archaeological evidence from other sources, and they have never caught him in a major error. To survive such critical scrutiny is a remarkable testimonial to a reporter who did not have the help of all the librarians, researchers, and sharp-eyed editors who keep watch over modern newsmen.

THE OUTSTANDING PASSAGES

While the whole book of Acts is highly readable, there are some outstanding passages which deserve particular attention. Among them are the following:

Peter preaches the first Christian sermon (Acts 2:14–42).

Execution of Stephen, the first Christian martyr (Acts 6:8–7:60).

How Ananias became the Father of Liars (Acts 5:1–11).

Philip meets an Ethiopian eunuch (Acts 8:26–40).

Conversion of Paul on the road to Damascus (Acts 9:1–43).

How Peter was convinced that Gentiles could be Christians, too (Acts 10:1–11:18).

What happened to a boy who fell asleep during a long sermon (Acts 20:7–12).

Paul's address to the scholarly Greeks of Athens (Acts 17:16–33).

Paul's party is caught in a storm and shipwrecked on the island of Malta (Acts 27:1–28:14).

THE GOSPEL ACCORDING TO JOHN

After reading Luke's account of the life of Christ and the history of the early Church, you may turn to the GOSPEL ACCORDING TO JOHN. Here you will find a different approach to the story. Whereas Luke is a reporter, John is a theologian. He is concerned not only with what happened, but also with *why* it happened and what it meant. He is especially intent on making clear who Jesus was, and in defining his relationship with God and his mission among men. Bishop Clement of Alexandria, one of the church fathers of the third century, aptly described John as "the spiritual gospel."

Very ancient tradition ascribes the authorship of this gospel to the Apostle John, who was Jesus' closest personal friend and the one to whom Jesus, when he was dying on the cross, commended his mother Mary for safekeeping. Some scholars think that the actual author may have been a disciple of John who recorded the apostle's memories. There is some internal evidence to support this view. John is clearly identified as the source of the material, but he is referred to in the third person. There also are a number of flattering references to him as "the disciple whom Jesus loved" which John himself might have hesitated to write in view of the lessons in humility which Jesus took such pains to teach him.

Regardless of who did the actual writing, the gospel clearly includes a great deal of firsthand, eyewitness testimony. It is full of homely little details, of no doctrinal significance, which could only have been supplied by someone who was there.

Some years ago, it was fashionable in some critical circles to cast doubt on the authenticity of John's gospel because it allegedly contained concepts and viewpoints which were too "Greek" to have come from a Jew of the first century A.D. This critical judgment has been quietly swept under the rug since the discovery of the Dead Sea Scrolls, which show that many of the same "Hellenistic" words and ideas were also being used by the Essene sect whose library was found in the caves near the village of Qumran on the Dead Sea. Radioactive carbon dating and archaeological evidence demonstrate conclusively that the Qumran sect flourished in the first century.

The prevailing view among scholars today is that the Gospel of John was written around A.D. 90, probably in the city of Ephesus. Both the date and place are consistent with apostolic origin, since other records of the early Church disclose that John lived to a very old age and died at Ephesus.

John's gospel presents many baffling problems to Biblical scholars, other than authorship. The other three gospels which are included in the New Testament canon—Matthew, Mark, and Luke—are in substantial agreement about the ministry of Jesus.° They deal primarily with things that Jesus said and did in his native province of Galilee, and mention only one trip to the capital city of Jerusalem, in the last week of his ministry. But John has Jesus going to Jerusalem on a number of occasions. John also differs in his chronology: for example, he says it was at the beginning rather than the end of his ministry that Jesus used a whip to drive the money-changers from the Temple.

Personally, I've never been able to get terribly excited about these differences. I suspect that if Biblical scholars had put in a little time editing copy on a news desk, they

---

° Hence they are known as the "synoptic gospels." One of the less familiar definitions of synoptic is "giving an account from the same point of view."

would marvel not at the relatively minor discrepancies among the various New Testament accounts of Christ's life, but rather at the great degree of harmony among them, particularly on the really important points. If UPI had four different reporters covering a running story that extended over as much time and territory as the life of Christ, we'd feel that they had done an extraordinarily good job if their accounts dovetailed as well as the gospels. And we certainly would not be surprised if one reporter came up with details which the other three didn't happen to have.

The most striking difference between John and the three synoptic gospels is in the way they present the teachings of Jesus. In all the synoptics, Jesus' teaching is usually given either in the form of parables or short, epigrammatic sayings. In John's gospel, on the other hand, we find long, philosophical discourses attributed to Jesus. Also, in the synoptics, Jesus says relatively little about himself, and even cautions his disciples not to go spreading the word around that he is the long-expected Messiah (because he knows that his "kingdom" is not the one the people are looking for). But John's account fairly bristles with statements in which Jesus boldly asserts that "I am the bread of life," "I am the good shepherd," and finally, "I and the Father are one . . . he who has seen me has seen the Father."

I must confess that these differences do bother me. Anyone with an ear for dialogue can tell that the Jesus of John's gospel does not sound like the Jesus of the synoptic gospels. John's version makes Jesus seem more didactic and argumentative, and less understanding and compassionate, than he is depicted by Luke and the other gospels. On the other hand, there are passages in the discourses recorded by John that are so brilliantly illuminating, so profound, so moving, that they *must* have come from Jesus. No ghost-writer could possibly have written them.

After wrestling with this quandary for a long time, I have concluded that there is only one satisfactory explanation. John was not as careful as a modern reporter is trained to be about distinguishing between a direct quote and an editorial comment. The long discourses which he records may thus contain both authentic words of Jesus and comments by John which are intended to elaborate, explain, or emphasize what John understood Jesus to mean. This was a common practice among writers of that day, and was not considered to be in any way improper.

A good example of what I'm talking about can be found in the third chapter of John's gospel. The first fifteen verses describe a conversation between Jesus and a Jewish leader named Nicodemus, who came by night to seek clarification of Jesus' teachings. Then follow six more verses which might be read either as a continuation of Jesus' remarks or as an interpolation by John warning against disbelief in Jesus. Some Bibles put the whole passage in quotes, but the Revised Standard Version ends the quotation marks after verse 15, which at least offers the reader a clue that the ensuing statements may be from John rather than from Jesus.

> Now there was a man of the Pharisees, named Nicodemus, a ruler of the Jews. This man came to Jesus by night and said to him, "Rabbi, we know that you are a teacher come from God; for no one can do these signs that you do, unless God is with him." Jesus answered him, "Truly, truly, I say to you, unless one is born anew, he cannot see the kingdom of God." Nicodemus said to him, "How can a man be born

when he is old? Can he enter a second time into his mother's womb and be born?" Jesus answered, "Truly, truly, I say to you, unless one is born of water and the Spirit, he cannot enter the kingdom of God. That which is born of the flesh is flesh, and that which is born of the Spirit is spirit. Do not marvel that I said to you, 'You must be born anew.' The wind blows where it wills, and you hear the sound of it, but you do not know whence it comes or whither it goes; so it is with every one who is born of the Spirit." Nicodemus said to him, "How can this be?" Jesus answered him, "Are you a teacher of Israel, and yet you do not understand this? Truly, truly, I say to you, we speak of what we know, and bear witness to what we have seen; but you do not receive our testimony. If I have told you earthly things and you do not believe, how can you believe if I tell you heavenly things? No one has ascended into heaven but he who descended from heaven, the Son of man. And as Moses lifted up the serpent in the wilderness, so must the Son of man be lifted up, that whoever believes in him may have eternal life."

For God so loved the world that he gave his only Son, that whoever believes in him should not perish but have eternal life. For God sent the Son into the world, not to condemn the world, but that the world might be saved through him. He who believes in him is not condemned; he who does not believe is condemned already, because he has not believed in the name of the only Son of God. And this is the judgment, that the light has come into the world, and men loved darkness rather than light, because their deeds were evil. For every one who does evil hates the light, and does not come to the light, lest his deeds should be exposed. But he who does what is true comes to the light, that it may be clearly seen that his deeds have been wrought in God.

John 3:1–21

I do not think it is necessary for the average reader to make a big thing of spotting all the passages in which John may have appended his own theological commentary to the Lord's words. But you may find it helpful, as I certainly have, to bear this possibility in mind whenever you encounter in John's gospel a statement which may seem to be attributed to Jesus but which strikes you as being too arrogant-sounding, harsh, or judgmental to have come from the humble, compassionate, and forgiving person whom we encounter in the other gospels and in other parts of John's own gospel.

HIGHLIGHTS TO WATCH FOR

You will want to read all of John's gospel, by all means. Here are some of the highlights to watch for:

The famous prologue, in the first fourteen verses of chapter 1, which expresses the mystery of the Incarnation in terms that no theologian has ever been able to improve upon.

Jesus turns water into wine at a wedding party to spare the host from embarrassment—a warmly human anecdote which stands as a perpetual rebuttal to the notion that Jesus was a blue-nosed ascetic (John 2:1–11).

Jesus drives the money-changers from the Temple (John 2:13–22). This story also corrects a widespread false impression of Jesus as a "meek and mild" fellow who never raised his voice or got angry.

The raising of Lazarus from the dead. This story is recorded only in John's gospel (John 11:1–44). It poses particular difficulties for those who automatically rule out miracles, because it does not read the least bit like a legend. On the contrary, it is full of little eyewitness touches and earthy details such as the objection which Lazarus' sister made when Jesus ordered the tomb unsealed: "He has been dead four days and by this time there will be a bad odor."

The great fourteenth chapter of John, which contains the whole Christian gospel in a nutshell. It affirms the promise of everlasting life in more moving terms than any other passage of Scripture—which is the reason why you've probably heard it many times at funeral services.

The fifteenth chapter, in which Jesus gives his disciples one last, overriding commandment: "that you love one another as I have loved you."

Jesus' prayer, shortly before his execution, that all of his followers "may be one"—the charter of the Christian unity movement (John 17:11).

An eyewitness account of the Crucifixion by one who stood at the foot of the cross in chapter 19 (don't overlook the poignant autobiographical note in verses 26 and 27).

An eyewitness account of the first Easter by one who looked into the empty tomb in chapter 20. (Again, note particularly the personal touch—years after the event, John is still proud that he outran Peter to the tomb.)

One word of caution, which applies to all the gospels but particularly to John: when you come across references to "the Jews" plotting against Jesus and seeking his destruction, remember that the writer is speaking about a specific and rather small minority of the population of Palestine—the leaders of the religious, social, and political establishment who looked upon Jesus as a dangerous revolutionary who was "stirring up the people" (as indeed he was). Many atrocious wrongs inflicted on Jews over the centuries might have been averted had Christians remembered that Jesus was executed precisely because the "common people"—that is, most of the Jews—"heard him gladly" and followed him in droves.

THE LETTERS OF JOHN

From the Gospel of John, skip to the three LETTERS OF JOHN, which you will find near the end of the New Testament. These brief letters, or "epistles" as they are called in the King James Version, are so similar in thought, literary style, and vocabulary to the Gospel of John that there can be very little doubt that they are by the same author. Like the gospel, they probably were written from Ephesus toward the end of the first century A.D.

The second and third letters (designated in Biblical shorthand as 2 John and 3 John) are not terribly important. They are very brief—thirteen verses in 2 John, and fifteen verses in 3 John—and are interesting primarily for the insight they give us into some of the troubles that beset the early Church.

But 1 John is a masterpiece. Nowhere in the Bible will you find the essence of Christianity expressed more succinctly or more eloquently. It, too, is relatively brief—only five chapters in all. It is not addressed to any particular church or individual, but to the whole Christian community. And its message is as timely today as it was nineteen centuries ago.

"Beloved, let us love one another," admonishes the old apostle. "He who does not love does not know God: for God is love."

I was one of the reporters sent to Little Rock, Arkansas, to cover the nation's first big desegregation crisis. On the Sunday morning after the paratroopers had moved in to quell street rioting, I attended worship services at one of Little Rock's largest churches. It had an overflow congregation, and on the faces of the worshipers you could read the whole gamut of human emotions—fear, anger, shame, puzzlement. The minister had obviously tried hard to rise to the occasion, but I cannot remember a word of his sermon. What I do remember vividly—and what I am sure many other members of the congregation will remember—is his text. It was 1 John 4:20, and it still strikes me as the perfect and complete answer to those who think that racism is compatible with Christianity: "If anyone says, 'I love God,' and hates his brother, he is a liar; for he who does not love his brother whom he has seen, cannot love God whom he has not seen."

There are many other passages of 1 John which are strikingly relevant to contemporary moral issues. For example, 1 John 3:17 seems to be aimed directly at church members who complain about the "burden" of foreign aid, or oppose domestic programs for elimination of poverty. John asks: "If any one has the world's goods and sees his brother in need, yet closes his heart against him, how does God's love abide in him?"

Not only does John warn that Christian faith must be accompanied by Christian action. He makes clear that the reverse is also true: human love is merely a refraction of God's love, and we are able to deal lovingly with our fellow man only to the extent that we are responsive to the love of God which was manifested in Jesus Christ. This

The Roman Empire
and Paul's Journeys

- - - - 1st JOURNEY
———— 2nd JOURNEY
.... 3rd JOURNEY

point is also remarkably apt for our own age, when some radical theologians are proclaiming the "death" of God and trying to promote a "religionless Christianity" based on purely human good will.

The second letter of John is addressed to "the elect lady and her children"—a metaphor meaning a local church and its members. We no longer know which local church received the letter, but from the internal evidence, we can surmise that it was one of the congregations in Asia Minor which were troubled during the latter years of the first century by the rise of the Gnostic heresy (see footnote on page 24). John warns the church against being misled by "deceivers" who "will not acknowledge the coming of Jesus Christ in the flesh." The Gnostics regarded all flesh as evil and therefore refused to believe that Christ had a true human body.

The third letter of John is addressed to an individual named Gaius, and is concerned with a long-forgotten internal row in a now-unknown local church. It is valuable primarily as a reminder to those who despair over contemporary divisions and dissensions that the Church has survived nearly 2000 years of this sort of thing. It would be hard to conceive of a more impressive testimony to the power of the Holy Spirit than the fact that the Church is still here after all these centuries of human squabbling.

THE LETTERS OF PAUL

A very large part of the New Testament—at least ten and possibly as many as thirteen of its twenty-seven books —came from the pen of a single writer, the apostle Paul.

Paul is one of the most fascinating figures in human history. As you know from reading the Acts of the Apostles, he was the leading missionary of the early Church, and the man primarily responsible for its rapid spread through the Roman Empire. He also was one of the first—and he still ranks as one of the best—Christian theologians. Few scholars would argue with the verdict of Alexander C. Purdy, Dean of Hartford Theological Seminary, that Paul "must be reckoned as second only to his Master Jesus Christ as a creative personality in Christianity."

He was born in the early years of the first century in the city of Tarsus, a rich and cosmopolitan trade center on the Mediterranean coast northwest of Syria. His parents were Diaspora Jews—that is, Jews living "in dispersion" beyond the boundaries of Palestine. They were devout in their faith and named their son Saul in honor of Israel's first king.

At an early age, Saul was sent to Jerusalem to study Jewish law under the great Rabbi Gamaliel. Like all students of his time, he learned a trade to support himself. His trade was tentmaking. Saul was an avid scholar. It was his nature to go all out in whatever he was doing. After a few years in rabbinical school, he had become a fiercely orthodox Jew and a member of the strictest sect of the Pharisees. He believed in dealing ruthlessly with all heresies. Although he may well have been in Jerusalem during Jesus' ministry, he said in later life that he never saw Jesus "in the flesh." It is not beyond the realm of possibility, however, that the rabid young Pharisee knew about the trial and execution of the "troublemaker" from Galilee, and if so, he doubtless approved heartily. We know, both from Acts and from his own writings, that he became one of the first persecutors of the infant Church, and was personally involved in the stoning of the first Christian martyr, Stephen.

His conversion is vividly described in the ninth chapter of Acts. "Saul, still breathing threats and murder against the disciples of the Lord, went to the high priest and asked him for letters to the synagogues of Damascus, so that if he found any (Christians) he might bring them bound to Jerusalem." But a strange thing happened to Saul on the way to Damascus. The risen Christ appeared to him and spoke to him. This was the last of the post-resurrection appearances recorded in the Bible, and it had a shattering impact on Saul of Tarsus. He became a Christian—possibly the most contagiously convinced Christian who ever lived. As a token of his spiritual rebirth, he changed his name to Paul.

For the next thirty years, until he died a martyr's death in Rome, Paul was a mainstay of the Church. He made three long missionary journeys through Asia Minor and Greece, founding Christian congregations wherever he went. At a critical time in the Church's history, when some of its leaders were content to let Christianity become just another sect within Judaism, Paul forcefully insisted on the universality of the faith. He called himself "the apostle to the Gentiles."

WHAT WE KNOW ABOUT PAUL

Paul was a man of enormous vitality and unflinching courage. He was once goaded by critics into listing some of the hardships he had endured as a missionary. Aside from his numerous imprisonments, he said, "Five times I have received at the hands of the Jews the forty lashes less one . . . Three times I have been beaten with rods . . . once I was stoned . . . Three times I have been shipwrecked." On his journeys, he encountered "danger from rivers, danger from robbers, danger from my own people, danger from Gentiles, danger in the city, danger in the wilderness, danger from false brethren." He suffered through "many a sleepless night in hunger and thirst, often without food, in cold and exposure."

Paul spent his last years in a Roman prison. He was beheaded in Rome in A.D. 64, during the savage persecution of Christians ordered by the Emperor Nero.

Tradition depicts Paul as a small, bald-headed, bow-legged man of unprepossessing appearance. He had some chronic ailment—perhaps epilepsy—which he referred to in his writings as "my thorn in the flesh." He prayed earnestly to be healed. But even though God gave him the power to heal others, Paul himself was never healed. It is a measure of Paul's great faith that he accepted this divine "no" without grumbling or self-pity. It is good to keep this fact in mind in reading Paul's letters. The unshakeable trust in the love of God which radiates from Paul's writing was not the fruit of a "happy" and secure life. It was in the midst of great suffering that Paul wrote, "I know whom I have believed. . . ."

Paul was a complex, many-sided person, and he reveals all of his contradictory facets to us in his letters. At times, he could be proud and boastful, almost to the point of arrogance. At other times, he was deeply humble. He had a quick temper, and could be quite harsh and sarcastic in replying to his critics. But he was also tenderhearted, magnanimous, and forgiving, and he obviously had a knack for making and keeping friends. He was keenly aware of his own shortcomings, and the painful knowledge that he could not overcome them by his own moral striving brought him to realize that man is utterly dependent on the grace of God. "I do not understand my own actions," Paul confessed in one of his letters. "For I do not do what I want, but I do the very thing I hate . . . I can will what is right, but I cannot do it."

In intellect as in personality, Paul was a man of sharp

contrasts. His writings display a number of prejudices which are so petty as to be almost laughable. He had a low opinion of women, and took a confirmed bachelor's jaundiced view of marriage. But his occasional streak of narrow-mindedness is a minor human flaw in an edifice of thought which has rarely been equaled and never surpassed for its breadth and brilliance. Paul is an authentic genius, and deserves a place on anyone's list of the ten greatest minds the human race has ever produced.

Judging from several allusions in his own letters, as well as a few cryptic hints in the book of Acts, Paul was not a very impressive public speaker. His forte was writing. Of all the New Testament writers, only Luke was a finer literary stylist. And some passages of Paul's letters, such as 1 Corinthians 13 and Romans 8, can hold their own among the world's greatest masterpieces of literature.

It is well to bear in mind that Paul had no idea that he was writing Holy Scripture. As he moved about in his missionary journeys, correspondence was the only method he had of keeping in touch with the young churches he had established. So he wrote letters. They were essentially business letters, in the sense that every one of them was written to deal with a specific situation. "Had telephones been invented," says Frederick C. Grant, Edward Robinson Professor Emeritus of Biblical Theology at Union Theological Seminary, "Paul certainly would have used them, and we should never have had any epistles from his pen."

THE OLDEST CHRISTIAN DOCUMENTS

It is possible that Paul wrote dozens of letters other than those which have been preserved in the New Testament. Instead of brooding over his lost letters, however, we should be grateful that so much of his writing was handed down to us. For Paul had no idea of writing for publication. His letters were intended to be read aloud in the churches to which they were addressed, and it would have been quite natural had they thereafter suffered the fate of most letters—namely, being thrown away. Instead, they were saved, and copied, and passed around to other churches. "It is surely a remarkable accident, if it is not the providence of God, that these human, unselfconscious letters of the very early days of Christianity should have been preserved," says J. B. Phillips, the English scholar who produced the Phillips translation of the Bible.

Aside from their intrinsic merit, which is great, Paul's letters have a special value as the oldest Christian documents extant.* Paul's first letter was written to the church at Thessalonica (Salonika in modern Greece) about A.D. 50. His last letters were written from Rome about A.D. 62. Thus, the whole body of Pauline writing was in existence before the first of the four gospels—Mark—was written, in about A.D. 68. On the rare instances when Paul covers the same ground as the gospel writers—for example, in his description of the institution of the Lord's Supper, or in his terse summary of Jesus' post-resurrection appearances— modern scholars unhesitatingly rely on Paul as the oldest written source.

But Paul does not devote much space to the life of Jesus. He was writing to people who were virtual contemporaries of Jesus and who had already heard from eye-witnesses all of the important facts of his ministry, death, and resurrection. Paul was intent on expounding the *meaning* of the mighty events which had so recently taken place in Palestine. His writings have retained an astonish-

* With the possible exception of the letter of James. See page 111.

ing relevance for every generation, including our own, because he addressed himself to the existential question: What does all this have to do with *me* and *my* life?

You may not like all of Paul's answers. His emphasis on God's righteous wrath and man's sinful condition are not congenial to an age which prefers to think of God as an indulgent Grandfather in Heaven, and which explains all human failings in terms of genes or environment. His insistence that man is powerless to save himself, and can be justified in the eyes of God only by an humble and penitent faith, is a jarring contradiction of the assumption that space-traveling, atom-splitting man can achieve anything he sets out to do. And his proclamation that salvation is to be found in Jesus Christ—and in Christ alone —seems rather illiberal to those who have been conditioned to equate tolerance with the notion that "one religion is as good as another."

If you find yourself boggling at Paul's uncompromising, 100-proof Christianity, it is a fairly sure sign that you have hitherto been exposed to what the late C. S. Lewis called "Christianity-and-water"—a diluted version which has been so thoroughly adapted to the intellectual prejudices of our time that it has lost all of the bite of the real thing. But hear Paul out, no matter how often he tramples on your pet preconceptions. It *could* be the unconscious mental attitudes which you have picked up from contemporary culture, rather than the Christian doctrines outlined by Paul, which are out of kilter.

THE LETTERS PAUL WROTE

The ten New Testament books which can be definitely attributed to Paul are Romans, 1 and 2 Corinthians, Galatians, Ephesians, Philippians, Colossians, 1 and 2 Thessalonians, and Philemon. They get their names from the addressees: thus Philippians is the letter Paul wrote to the church at Philippi, a city in Macedonia.

The authorship of three so-called "pastoral letters"—1 and 2 Timothy and Titus—is disputed. They purport to be from Paul's hand, and each of them opens with his familiar salutation, "Paul, an apostle of Jesus Christ. . . ." They are addressed to two younger men, Timothy and Titus, who had served under Paul on his missionary journeys. They are called "pastoral" letters because they contain fatherly advice from a veteran pastor to neophytes in the ministry.

Some critics assert that these three letters differ so greatly in vocabulary and literary style from Paul's other letters that they cannot have been written by the apostle. They postulate that the author was a disciple of Paul, writing after the apostle's death, and perhaps incorporating some fragments of genuine Pauline letters. If this thesis is accepted, it does not mean that the unknown author was a forger or perpetrator of fraud. It was a widespread and accepted practice of that day for a disciple to attribute his own literary efforts to his master.

Other Biblical scholars, including the great Karl Barth, are convinced that Paul himself wrote the pastoral letters. The debate has been going on for many years, and turns on such recondite questions as the frequency with which certain Greek verbs appear. Without having the credentials to enter this argument, I can only offer a layman's untutored opinion that the pastorals sound like the kind of letters Paul might have written to young friends when he was old and tired and awaiting execution.

Paul's letters are not arranged in the New Testament in chronological order, or any other logical sequence. They appear rather in an order which seems to appeal to people of the Middle East (it is also found in the Koran), namely, in order of their length. The longest (Romans) comes first, the shortest (Philemon) last.

BEGIN WITH THESSALONIANS

You can read them as you find them in your Bible, if you wish. But I think you'll get more out of them if you rearrange them in a somewhat more logical order.

I suggest starting with 1 and 2 THESSALONIANS, which are the first letters Paul wrote. They are not particularly profound, and they contain little of the theological brilliance which marks Paul's mature work. But they do reveal a great deal about his fatherly concern for the young churches he had established, a concern expressed now in warm words of praise and encouragement, and again in stern admonitions and rebukes. They also demonstrate Paul's tendency—which is even more pronounced in his later letters—to shift abruptly from abstract doctrinal questions to exceedingly practical problems of everyday living.

Thessalonica was the capital of Macedonia. Paul established a church there on his second missionary journey, after being driven out of nearby Philippi (see 1 Thessalonians 2:2). In Thessalonica, as well, he encountered violent opposition from members of the city's large Jewish community. He was finally forced to leave, and the little congregation of Christians he left behind him was subjected to an intense barrage of propaganda, designed to discredit Paul's character and motives. Paul sent his colleague Timothy back to Thessalonica to encourage the infant church to hold firm. Later, after arriving in Corinth about A.D. 50, the apostle himself wrote the letter which we call 1 Thessalonians. In it, Paul defends himself against his critics, pointing out, among other things, that he did not take any money for preaching but earned his own living (as a tentmaker) while living among them. He also answers two questions which the Thessalonians had asked Timothy to clear up for them: When will Christ return? and What happens to Christians who die before his Second Coming?

It was widely believed among first century Christians that Jesus would return almost any day. Paul himself shared the view that it probably would not be long before the Lord returned in glory to subdue all the world to his reign. But he warned the Thessalonians (1 Thessalonians 5:1–11) that "the day of the Lord will come like a thief in the night"—in other words, no one really knows when to expect it.

This admonition evidently did not sink in. In 2 Thessalonians, written from Corinth about a year later, we find Paul rebuking members of the Christian community who have quit work and are "living in idleness" because they think that the Second Coming is imminent. The apostle offers forthright advice for dealing with this attitude: "If anyone will not work, let him not eat."

GALATIANS

After reading Paul's letters to the Thessalonians (which won't take long, since both are very brief), you can ease into somewhat deeper water with GALATIANS.

This is a passionately angry letter which Paul wrote about A.D. 55, probably from Corinth. It is addressed to all the churches of Galatia, a province of Asia Minor which included such important cities as Antioch, Lystra, and Iconium. Paul had established a number of churches in Galatia during his second missionary journey. After his departure, however, the churches came under the influence of "Judaizing" teachers who contended that Christians, in addition to having faith in Jesus Christ, must keep the Mosaic law. In his letter, Paul denounces this doctrine with his customary forthrightness: "O foolish Galatians, who has bewitched you?"

The letter to the Galatians is sometimes called "the Magna Carta of Christian liberty" because in it, Paul lays down the doctrine that "a man is not justified by works of the law but through faith in Jesus Christ."

"Christ has set us free," Paul proclaims, from the tyranny of legalistic religion, from ritualistic observances such as circumcision, and from the whole endeavor to "earn" salvation through good works.

But Christian liberty does not mean license to "gratify the desires of the flesh." For those who are "called to freedom" in Christ are subject to a higher law—the law of love. They have only one guide for conduct—to live and act in the Spirit of Christ.

Paul spells it out in a memorable passage of Galatians 5:

> For you were called to freedom, brethren; only do not use your freedom as an opportunity for the flesh, but through love be servants of one another. For the whole law is fulfilled in one word, "You shall love your neighbor as yourself." But if you bite and devour one another take heed that you are not consumed by one another.
>
> But I say, walk by the Spirit, and do not gratify the desires of the flesh. For the desires of the flesh are against the Spirit, and the desires of the Spirit are against the flesh; for these are opposed to each other, to prevent you from doing what you would. But if

you are led by the Spirit you are not under the law. Now the works of the flesh are plain: immorality, impurity, licentiousness, idolatry, sorcery, enmity, strife, jealousy, anger, selfishness, dissension, party spirit, envy, drunkenness, carousing, and the like. I warn you, as I warned you before, that those who do such things shall not inherit the kingdom of God. But the fruit of the Spirit is love, joy, peace, patience, kindness, goodness, faithfulness, gentleness, self-control; against such there is no law. And those who belong to Christ Jesus have crucified the flesh with its passions and desires.

If we live by the Spirit, let us also walk by the Spirit. Let us have no self-conceit, no provoking of one another, no envy of one another.

Galatians 5:13–26

"The importance of this brief letter is hard to overestimate," says Bruce M. Metzger. "The declaration of principles set forth in these six chapters made Christianity a world religion instead of a Jewish sect."

Galatians also has biographical interest (Paul rambles on at some length about his early life) and provides valuable historical information about the early Church.

Finally, it includes one unforgettable sentence which stands in perpetual judgment over any church that practices or condones segregation: "There is neither Jew nor Greek, there is neither slave nor free, there is neither male nor female: for you are all one in Christ Jesus" (Galatians 3:28).

NOW YOU ARE READY FOR ROMANS

After warming up with Galatians, you are ready to tackle Paul's longest and greatest letter—ROMANS.

This letter was written about A.D. 56, probably from Corinth. It is addressed to the church at Rome—a church which Paul did not found and which, at the time of writing, he had never even visited. It is polite, even deferential, in tone compared to the pastoral admonitions he was accustomed to fire off to his own little flocks in Asia Minor and Greece. Paul hoped to get to Rome soon (as he mentions in Romans 1:10–13), and he sent the letter ahead of him as a sort of introduction. He knew that the Roman Christians would have heard a lot about him, including some scurrilous libels spread by his opponents, and he wanted to give them a firsthand account of his beliefs. Being a little vain about his intellectual ability—as he had every right to be—he may also have had a secret urge to show the people in the Big City that he was no country preacher, but could hold his own with any Greek or Roman philosopher.

The result, in the words of Robert C. Dentan of Berkeley Divinity School, was "one of the most profound and influential documents in all the literature of the world."

Martin Luther found in the letter to the Romans many of the basic ideas of the Protestant Reformation. Centuries later, in our own time, Karl Barth launched another theological revolution with a *Commentary on the Epistle to the Romans*.

The first eight chapters of Romans present a single sustained argument, which is really an elaboration of the doctrine of "justification by faith" which Paul expounded, more succinctly, in his letter to the Galatians. These chapters are not easy reading, but they deserve the most careful study.

Paul begins by describing the sins to which men seem to be hopelessly addicted. He warns that "the judgment of God rightly falls upon those who do such things," and

—in a sentence that very much needs hearing in our day
—cautions against "presuming upon" God's patience by
failing to recognize how ugly our sins must be in his sight.

He says that men are powerless to save themselves by
good works, or by meticulous devotion to laws and religious rituals. "*All* have sinned and fallen short of the
glory of God," and the only One who can save them is the
same God whom they have offended. And this is just what
God in His infinite mercy has seen fit to do. Sinful men
have been "justified"—that is, made acceptable in the sight
of God—"by his grace as a gift." And the agency of their
redemption is Jesus Christ. For "while we were yet helpless . . . Christ died for the ungodly." Christ's death
achieved a "reconciliation" between righteous God and
sinful man—and peace with God will henceforth be forever available to all who trust in Christ.

PAUL AT HIS VERY BEST

Paul's discourse reaches a climax in the eighth chapter
of Romans, which summarizes all that he has been trying
to say. This is one of the greatest chapters of the whole
Bible. I cannot resist the temptation to quote it in full as a
sample of Paul at his very best:

> There is therefore now no condemnation for those
> who are in Christ Jesus. For the law of the Spirit of
> life in Christ Jesus has set me free from the law of
> sin and death. For God has done what the law, weak-
> ened by the flesh, could not do: sending his own Son
> in the likeness of sinful flesh and for sin, he con-
> demned sin in the flesh, in order that the just require-
> ment of the law might be fulfilled in us, who walk
> not according to the flesh but according to the Spirit.
> For those who live according to the flesh set their

minds on the things of the flesh, but those who live according to the Spirit set their minds on the things of the Spirit. To set the mind on the flesh is death, but to set the mind on the Spirit is life and peace. For the mind that is set on the flesh is hostile to God; it does not submit to God's law, indeed it cannot; and those who are in the flesh cannot please God.

But you are not in the flesh, you are in the Spirit, if the spirit of God really dwells in you. Anyone who does not have the spirit of Christ does not belong to him. But if Christ is in you, although your bodies are dead because of sin, your spirits are alive because of righteousness. If the Spirit of him who raised Jesus from the dead dwells in you, he who raised Christ Jesus from the dead will give life to your mortal bodies also through his Spirit which dwells in you.

So then, brethren, we are debtors, not to the flesh, to live according to the flesh—for if you live according to the flesh you will die, but if by the Spirit you put to death the deeds of the body you will live. For all who are led by the Spirit of God are sons of God. For you did not receive the spirit of slavery to fall back into fear, but you have received the spirit of sonship. When we cry, "Abba! Father!" it is the Spirit himself bearing witness with our spirit that we are children of God, and if children, then heirs, heirs of God and fellow heirs with Christ, provided we suffer with him in order that we may also be glorified with him.

I consider that the sufferings of this present time are not worth comparing with the glory that is to be revealed to us. For the creation waits with eager longing for the revealing of the sons of God; for the creation was subjected to futility, not of its own will but by the will of him who subjected it in hope; because the creation itself will be set free from its bondage to decay and obtain the glorious liberty of the children of God. We know that the whole creation has been groaning in travail together until now; and not only the creation, but we ourselves, who have the first fruits of the Spirit, groan inwardly as we wait for adoption as sons, the redemption of our bodies. For in this hope we are saved. Now hope that is seen is not hope. For who hopes for what he sees? But if we hope for what we do not see, we wait for it with patience.

Likewise the Spirit helps us in our weakness; for we do not know how to pray as we ought, but the Spirit himself intercedes for us with sighs too deep for words. And he who searches the hearts of men knows what is the mind of the Spirit, because the Spirit intercedes for the saints according to the will of God.

We know that in everything God works for good with those who love him, who are called according to his purpose. For those whom he foreknew he also predestined to be conformed to the image of his Son, in order that he might be the first-born among many brethren. And those whom he predestined he also called; and those whom he called he also justified; and those whom he justified he also glorified.

What then shall we say to this? If God is for us, who is against us? He who did not spare his own Son but gave him up for us all, will he not also give us all things with him? Who shall bring any charge against God's elect? It is God who justifies; who is to condemn? Is it Christ Jesus, who died, yes, who was raised from the dead, who is at the right hand of God, who indeed intercedes for us? Who shall separate us from the love of Christ? Shall tribulation, or distress, or persecution, or famine, or nakedness, or peril, or sword? As it is written,

"For thy sake we are being killed all the day long;
we are regarded as sheep to be slaughtered."

No, in all these things we are more than conquerors through him who loved us. For I am sure that neither death, nor life, nor angels, nor principalities, nor things present, nor things to come, nor powers, nor height, nor depth, nor anything else in all creation, will be able to separate us from the love of God in Christ Jesus our Lord."

Romans 8

In chapters 9 through 11, Paul wrestles with the question of what will become of "Old" Israel—the Jews who did not accept Christ. Speaking as an Israelite who is proud of his ancestry, he warns Gentiles not to assume that God has "rejected" his chosen people. He voices his fervent prayer that all Jews eventually will turn to Christ. One wonders how many anti-Semitic atrocities of the past 1900 years might have been averted if Christians in every generation had read Paul's words and taken them to heart.

The eleventh chapter, by the way, contains one of the most provocative sentences in all of Paul's letters—"Behold the kindness and the severity of God." It is rarely taken as a text for sermons today. We prefer to think of God's kindness; the thought that He can also be severe in His judgment of unrepentant sinners is a bit disturbing.

The thirteenth chapter has caused quite a lot of controversy through the centuries. Only a few years ago, it figured in a transatlantic row between two theological giants, Karl Barth and Reinhold Niebuhr, over the proper attitude of Christians (such as those in East Germany) toward a Communist government. Paul lays down the rule that Christians should always "be subject to the governing authorities," and suggests that all civil authority is derived from God.

I think the best way to come to terms with this chapter is to remember that Paul was writing to the capital of the empire, and that he was eager to assure the Roman authorities that Christians were not a subversive sect. It should also be remembered that when the chips were down, some years later, Paul himself defied the civil authority of the Roman government by refusing to worship the Emperor, and paid for this defiance with his life, as did thousands of his fellow Christians in Rome. To use Romans 13 as an argument against Christian resistance to oppression 2000 years later is to put far more weight on Paul's remarks about civil authority than he evidently did.

The letter closes with typically Pauline admonitions about how to live a Christian life, and with a long list of personal greetings, which remind us that this classic presentation of Christian doctrine was never conceived as a theological treatise, but was simply a letter from one first-century Christian to some of his brethren.

CORINTHIANS

My personal favorite among Paul's letters is 1 CORIN-THIANS. It was written while Paul was living in the city of Ephesus, possibly as early as A.D. 54, but more likely around 56 or 57. It is addressed to the church at Corinth, which had been founded by Paul a few years earlier. Corinth was directly across the Aegean from Ephesus, and was the fourth largest city of the Roman Empire (being surpassed by Rome, Alexandria, and Ephesus, in that order). Originally Greek, Corinth had, by the first century A.D., become a polyglot metropolis like modern New York City, with large numbers of Italians, Egyptians, Syrians, Orientals, and Jews in its population. Its people were highly sophisticated and their lax moral standards were notorious throughout the Empire. "To live like a Corinthian" was a proverbial expression for dissolute conduct. One of the most thriving religious sects was the cult of the Greek goddess Aphrodite, which had 1000 priestess-prostitutes on the staff of its temple.

The letter we call "First Corinthians" is not actually the first which Paul wrote to the church at Corinth. He refers (1 Corinthians 5:9) to an earlier letter, which unhappily was not preserved. In this letter, Paul is concerned, as always, with immediate practical problems. First, he rebukes the Corinthians for factionalism, which has divided the little congregation into cliques, some loyal to Paul, others to a missionary named Apollos, who followed Paul as spiritual leader of the Corinthian church. Paul makes a stirring plea for unity which is fully as timely today as it was nineteen centuries ago:

> I appeal to you, brethren, by the name of our Lord Jesus Christ, that all of you agree and that there be no dissensions among you, but that you be united in the same mind and the same judgment.
>
> 1 Corinthians 1:10

He also reprimands the Corinthians for tolerating gross sexual immorality in their midst, and for dragging each other into the law courts to settle their differences (see chapters 5 and 6).

Then, in chapter 7, he undertakes to answer questions

which the Corinthians have put to him in a letter. The
first question concerns marriage, and Paul's reply leaves
no room for doubt about his very dim view of the whole
institution. His bachelor bias against matrimony is rein-
forced by his belief that the end of the world is fast ap-
proaching, so it is no time for anyone to be making basic
changes in his way of life. It is interesting to note that
Paul realizes and admits that he is voicing his own opinion, and not the command of Christ.

Now concerning the unmarried, I have no command of the Lord, but I give my opinion as one who
by the Lord's mercy is trustworthy. I think that in
view of the impending distress it is well for a person
to remain as he is. Are you bound to a wife? Do not
seek to be free. Are you free from a wife? Do not
seek marriage. But if you marry, you do not sin, and
if a girl marries she does not sin. Yet those who
marry will have worldly troubles, and I would spare
you that. I mean, brethren, the appointed time has
grown very short; from now on, let those who have
wives live as though they had none, and those who
mourn as though they were not mourning, and those
who rejoice as though they were not rejoicing, and
those who buy as though they had no goods, and
those who deal with the world as though they had
no dealings with it. For the form of this world is
passing away.

I want you to be free from anxieties. The unmarried man is anxious about the affairs of the Lord,
how to please the Lord; but the married man is
anxious about worldly affairs, how to please his wife,
and his interests are divided. And the unmarried
woman or girl is anxious about the affairs of the

Lord, how to be holy in body and spirit; but the married woman is anxious about worldly affairs, how to please her husband. I say this for your own benefit, not to lay any restraint upon you, but to promote good order and to secure your undivided devotion to the Lord.

If any one thinks that he is not behaving properly toward his betrothed, if his passions are strong, and it has to be, let him do as he wishes: let them marry —it is no sin. But whoever is firmly established in his heart, being under no necessity but having his desire under control, and has determined this in his heart, to keep her as his betrothed, he will do well. So that he who marries his betrothed does well; and he who refrains from marriage will do better.

1 Corinthians 7:25-38

MARRIAGE AND WOMEN

Although we are inclined today to smile at Paul's prejudices against marriage, it is only fair to note that one of his arguments for the single state is based not on his crotchety dislike of women, but on his fervent desire to serve Christ. "The unmarried man is anxious about the affairs of the Lord, how to please the Lord," he says. "But the married man is anxious about worldly affairs, how to please his wife." Every husband must admit there's some truth to that statement. The Catholic Church takes Paul's admonition very seriously: it is the basic reason for the disciplinary rule requiring Roman priests to remain celibate.

In chapters 8, 9, and 10, Paul deals with a question which was very important to members of a young church living in a pagan culture, but which may seem at first glance to be totally irrelevant to modern Christians. The question is whether it is all right for a Christian to eat food which has been "offered to idols"—that is, consecrated in a pagan temple. Much of the meat sold in the market places of Corinth came from animals sacrificed in pagan rites. Some Christians had moral scruples about eating such meat. Others felt that it was perfectly lawful for a Christian to eat any kind of meat, so long as he recognized that "an idol has no real existence."

Paul's answer demonstrates his genius for dealing with every human problem in terms of timeless and universal principles. Of course, he says, it is lawful for a Christian to "eat whatever is sold in the meat market without raising any question on the ground of conscience." But a Christian should be concerned not only with what is lawful for him, but also with what is "helpful" to his brother. If eating meat that has been consecrated in pagan temples causes some of the less sophisticated Christians to "stumble"—that is, to slip back into idol worship—then the more knowledgeable members of the church should refrain from the practice. "Let no one seek his own good, but the good of his neighbor." It is a measure of Paul's continuing influence that the Methodist Church today bases its case for abstinence from alcohol primarily on this passage of Scripture. The argument is that Christians who can drink in moderation should nevertheless forego alcohol for the sake of others who may be more susceptible to excess.

In chapter 11, Paul lays down the rule that women should keep their heads covered in church. It is still meekly obeyed by millions of women, of whom relatively few, I suspect, are aware that it stemmed originally from a misogynous desire to emphasize woman's inferiority to man.

The real meat in chapter 11, however, is found in verses 23 to 26. Here you will find the oldest record of the institution of the Lord's Supper—written more than twenty years before any of the gospels. The reverence which the Church has always accorded this ancient witness is reflected in the fact that nearly all Christian bodies —Catholic, Protestant, Anglican, and Orthodox—use the exact words which Paul quotes Jesus as having used in consecrating the bread and wine of the Eucharist.

For I received from the Lord what I also delivered to you, that the Lord Jesus on the night when he was betrayed took bread, and when he had given thanks, he broke it, and said, "This is my body which is for you. Do this in remembrance of me." In the same way also the cup, after supper, saying, "This cup is the new covenant in my blood. Do this, as often as you drink it, in remembrance of me." For as often as you eat this bread and drink the cup, you proclaim the Lord's death until he comes.

1 Corinthians 11:23–26

In chapter 12, Paul uses a striking metaphor to describe the Church. It is "the Body of Christ" and each of its members has a particular role to perform, just as each member of the human body has its special part to play. This concept of the Church has been rediscovered by Protestants and Catholics alike in recent years, and has become the basis for the new emphasis on the ministry of the laity which is one of the most healthful trends in the religious life of the twentieth century.

DIVINE LOVE

Chapter 13 is the best-known and best-loved passage that Paul ever wrote. It is the apostle's lyric description of love—not the erotic love which was all too familiar to the Corinthians, but the new kind of selfless, compassionate concern for others which characterized the Christian fellowship at its best. To designate this special kind of Christian love, Paul adopted a Greek word which had hitherto been rarely used in first-century literature—*agape*. The King James Version tries to capture the flavor of *agape* by translating it "charity." Modern translations render it "love" which is more accurate if we can dissociate the English word from some of the connotations it has picked up in Hollywood and Tin Pan Alley.

If I speak in the tongues of men and of angels, but have not love, I am a noisy gong or a clanging cymbal. And if I have prophetic powers, and understand all mysteries and all knowledge, and if I have all faith, so as to remove mountains, but have not love, I am nothing. If I give away all I have, and if I deliver my body to be burned, but have not love, I gain nothing.

Love is patient and kind; love is not jealous or boastful; it is not arrogant or rude. Love does not insist on its own way; it is not irritable or resentful; it does not rejoice at wrong, but rejoices in the right. Love bears all things, believes all things, hopes all things, endures all things.

Love never ends; as for prophecy, it will pass away; as for tongues, they will cease; as for knowledge, it will pass away. For our knowledge is imperfect and our prophecy is imperfect; but when the perfect comes, the imperfect will pass away. When I was a child, I reasoned like a child; when I became a man, I gave up childish ways. For now we see in a mirror dimly, but then face to face. Now I know in

part; then I shall understand fully, even as I have
been fully understood. So faith, hope, love abide,
these three; but the greatest of these is love.

1 Corinthians 13

After this magnificent passage, Paul would seem
doomed to descend to anti-climax. But he doesn't. The
letter ends (chapter 15) with Paul's incomparable discussion of the Resurrection. In 1 Corinthians 15:3–8 we
have the earliest written record of Christ's post-
Resurrection appearances. Writing when many of the eyewitnesses were still alive and available to corroborate or
challenge his testimony, Paul unhesitatingly affirms that
the Resurrection was a real, historical event, not a
"spiritual episode" in the minds of the disciples. He is
willing, in fact, to stake the whole case for Christianity
on the flat assertion that this incredible thing actually
happened.

For I delivered to you as of first importance what
I also received, that Christ died for our sins in accordance with the scriptures, that he was buried,
that he was raised on the third day in accordance
with the scriptures, and that he appeared to Cephas,
then to the twelve. Then he appeared to more than
five hundred brethren at one time, most of whom
are still alive, though some have fallen asleep. Then
he appeared to James, then to all the apostles. Last
of all, as to one untimely born, he appeared also to
me. . . .

Now if Christ is preached as raised from the dead,
how can some of you say that there is no resurrection
of the dead? But if there is no resurrection of the
dead, then Christ has not been raised; if Christ has

not been raised, then our preaching is in vain and your faith is in vain. We are even found to be misrepresenting God, because we testified of God that he raised Christ, whom he did not raise if it is true that the dead are not raised. For if the dead are not raised, then Christ has not been raised. If Christ has not been raised, your faith is futile and you are still in your sins. Then those also who have fallen asleep in Christ have perished. If in this life we who are in Christ have only hope, we are of all men most to be pitied.

But in fact Christ has been raised from the dead, the first fruits of those who have fallen asleep. For as by a man came death, by a man has come also the resurrection of the dead. For as in Adam all die, so also in Christ shall all be made alive.

1 Corinthians 15:3–8; 12–22

Later in the same chapter, Paul answers a question that is often put to pastors today:

But some one will ask, "How are the dead raised? With what kind of body do they come?" You foolish man! What you sow does not come to life unless it dies. And what you sow is not the body which is to be, but a bare kernel, perhaps of wheat or of some other grain. But God gives it a body as he has chosen, and to each kind of seed its own body. For not all flesh is alike, but there is one kind for men, another for animals, another for birds, and another for fish. There are celestial bodies and there are terrestrial bodies; but the glory of the celestial is one, and the glory of the terrestrial is another. There is one glory of the sun, and another glory of the moon, and another glory of the stars; for star differs from star in glory.

So is it with the resurrection of the dead. What is sown is perishable, what is raised is imperishable. It is sown in dishonor, it is raised in glory. It is sown in weakness, it is raised in power. It is sown a physical body, it is raised a spiritual body. If there is a physical body, there is also a spiritual body. Thus it is written, "The first man Adam became a living being"; the last Adam became a life-giving spirit. But it is not the spiritual which is first but the physical, and then the spiritual. The first man was from the earth, a man of dust; the second man is from heaven. As was the man of dust, so are those who are of the dust; and as is the man of heaven, so are those who are of heaven. Just as we have borne the image of the man of dust, we shall also bear the image of the man of heaven. I tell you this, brethren: flesh and blood cannot inherit the kingdom of God, nor does the perishable inherit the imperishable.

Lo! I tell you a mystery. We shall not all sleep, but we shall all be changed, in a moment, in the twinkling of an eye, at the last trumpet. For the trumpet will sound, and the dead will be raised imperishable, and we shall be changed. For this perishable nature must put on the imperishable, and this mortal nature must put on immortality. When the perishable puts on the imperishable, and the mortal puts on immortality, then shall come to pass the saying that is written:

> "Death is swallowed up in victory."
> "O death, where is thy victory?
> O death, where is thy sting."

The sting of death is sin, and the power of sin is the law. But thanks be to God, who gives us the victory through our Lord Jesus Christ.

1 Corinthians 15:35–57

The letter called 2 CORINTHIANS was written from Ephesus about a year after 1 Corinthians. In the meantime, Paul's relations with the congregation at Corinth have been strained, and he has made a "painful visit" to his former flock to try to straighten things out. He has also written an angry letter (now lost) in which he apparently said some harsh things he now regrets. To make amends, he sent his young assistant, Titus, to visit the Corinthians, and Titus has returned, bringing good news of a rapprochement. The first nine chapters of 2 Corinthians reveal Paul's delight and gratitude at being restored to friendly terms with his beloved but often unruly "children" in Corinth.

Highlights include:

2 Corinthians 4:16–18, in which Paul expresses his faith that the sufferings of this life are nothing compared to the glory that awaits us.

2 Corinthians 5:19, the often-quoted sentence which sums up the whole doctrine of the Incarnation: "God was in Christ reconciling the world to himself."

The last four chapters (10 through 13) of the letter are so radically different in tone that many scholars believe that they are a misplaced fragment of another letter—perhaps the angry letter referred to previously. Here we see Paul in his worst light—defending himself against criticism by boasting of his own record as an apostle. The only redeeming feature of this tirade is Paul's reiterated confession—which keeps breaking into his boasting—that he is making a fool of himself. He knows it, and still he does it. We instinctively want to turn away from the spectacle in embarrassment for him. But we should remember that it was Paul's very human weaknesses—and his keen awareness of them—which led him to recognize the central truth of all his preaching: we are saved not because we are good and deserving, but because God is merciful and forgiving.

EPHESIANS

The letter which we call EPHESIANS was written about A.D. 62, while Paul was in prison in Rome. Unlike his other letters, it contains no allusions to individuals or to local situations. This fact has prompted scholars to conclude that it was probably an encyclical or circular letter, addressed to a number of churches in Asia Minor. According to this thesis, the copy which went to the church at Ephesus happened to be the one which was preserved and which later found its way into the New Testament canon. Hence it was known from very early times as the Ephesians' letter.

It is a relatively brief letter, and contains no doctrine or teaching that cannot be found elsewhere in Paul's writings. But it is well worth reading, for it says several important things more clearly and more memorably than Paul managed to say them anywhere else.

Be sure to note:

Ephesians 2:4–9, in which Paul expounds his favorite theme that our salvation is not our own doing, but an undeserved gift from God.

Ephesians 3:14–20, one of the most beautiful prayers in the whole library of Christian devotion.

Ephesians 4:31–32, Paul's prescription for Christian fellowship: "Be kind to one another, tenderhearted, forgiving one another, as God in Christ forgave you."

Ephesians 5:22–33, in which Paul instructs wives to be obedient to their husbands, and husbands to love their wives.

Ephesians 6:1–4, his counsel on parent-child relationships.

Ephesians 6:10–17, the famous passage about putting on the whole armor of God, which preachers like to use as a text for sermons.

PHILIPPIANS

PHILIPPIANS also was a product of Paul's prison days in Rome. It is addressed to the first church which Paul founded in Europe—at the city of Philippi in Macedonia. It is the most gentle and gracious of Paul's letters, and much of it is devoted to expressing his gratitude for the kindness which the Philippians have shown to him during his imprisonment.

Its most important passage is found in chapter 2, verses 5 through 11. Here, with a marvelous economy of words, Paul lays down a doctrine concerning the person of Christ. It is sometimes called the "kenotic" doctrine from a Greek word meaning self-emptying, and you will see when you read it why the term is appropriate. No higher tribute can be paid to Paul's genius as a religious philosopher than the fact that lesser theologians have written literally hundreds of books during the past twenty years elaborating on and "interpreting" the doctrine which he expresses, quite clearly and adequately, in little more than 100 words.

Here is the full text of this great passage:

Have this mind among yourselves, which you have in Christ Jesus, who, though he was in the form of God, did not count equality with God a thing to be grasped, but emptied himself, taking the form of a servant, being born in the likeness of men. And being found in human form he humbled himself and became obedient unto death, even death on a cross. Therefore God has highly exalted him and bestowed on him the name which is above every name, that at the name of Jesus every knee should bow, in heaven and on earth and under the earth, and every tongue confess that Jesus Christ is Lord, to the glory of God the Father.

Philippians 2:5–11

Another noteworthy passage is Philippians 4:4–7, in which Paul speaks with authority about the joy and serenity of being a Christian, and of "the peace of God, which passes all understanding." This little outburst of sheer happiness is doubly moving if you bear in mind that it was written by a man who was old, sick, tired, in prison, and awaiting execution.

Rejoice in the Lord always; again I will say, Rejoice. Let all men know your forbearance. The Lord is at hand. Have no anxiety about anything, but in everything by prayer and supplication with thanksgiving let your requests be made known to God. And the peace of God, which passes all understanding, will keep your hearts and your minds in Christ Jesus.

Philippians 4:4–7

COLOSSIANS

COLOSSIANS is another of Paul's "prison letters," written from Rome between A.D. 62 and 64. It is addressed to the church at Colossae, a town in Asia Minor which was noted primarily for its textile industry. One of Paul's missionary assistants, Epaphras, had founded a church there, but there is no evidence that the apostle himself ever visited Colossae. His letter to the infant church was prompted by reports that the congregation was being led astray by "false teachers." We cannot now tell precisely what heresy was troubling the Colossians, but it was apparently one of the "mystery religion" cults which abounded in the Roman Empire during the first century. This would account for Paul's repeated references to Christ as the one in whom "the mystery" of God's will and purposes has been "made manifest" to all mankind. What he is saying is that all of the truth that matters has been revealed to men through Christ, and no one needs to dabble in esoteric rites or seek "inside information" to be saved.

Chapter 3 is of greatest interest to contemporary readers. It is a classic example of Paul's penchant for giving moral instruction by listing good things on one hand, and bad things on the other hand.

THE LETTERS TO PHILEMON,
TIMOTHY, AND TITUS

The LETTER TO PHILEMON is a brief, purely personal bit of correspondence which was never intended to be published. It demonstrates that Paul, for all his fiery temper, was an exceptionally kind and thoughtful person. A slave named Onesimus robbed his master, Philemon, and ran away from his home in Colossae. In time, Onesimus made his way to Rome, where he became a convert to Christianity and a devoted disciple of Paul. Under Roman law, a runaway slave was subject to prompt execution if caught. Or he could be subjected to any other punishment his master desired. Paul made discreet inquiries and discovered that the master, Philemon, had also become a Christian and a member of the church at Colossae. So Paul sent Onesimus home (thus getting him out of the dangerous category of runaway) with a letter urging Philemon to receive him "not now as a servant," but as "a brother beloved."

"For love's sake, I appeal to you—I Paul, an ambassador and now a prisoner also for Christ Jesus—I appeal to you for my child, Onesimus. . . ."

It is an irresistibly gracious letter, and even contains one of Paul's rare flashes of humor: the remark in verse 11 about Onesimus having been *useless* but now returning to be *useful*, although it makes little sense in English, was a rather good pun in Greek, because Onesimus is the Greek word for *useful*.

"Receive him as you would receive me," says Paul. "If he has wronged you at all, or owes you anything, charge that to my account."

We don't know how the story came out, but it is impossible to believe that Philemon could have rejected such a plea.

The two LETTERS TO TIMOTHY, as noted above, have become a subject of controversy as regards who wrote them, and when, and to whom. If we take them at face value, they were written by Paul during the last years of his life to his young colleague, Timothy.

One thing can be said for certain: if the author was not Paul, he certainly shared Paul's prejudices against women. I have often quoted 1 Timothy 2:11 to my wife, but I cannot say that it has been warmly received.* As for the author's admonitions about how women should dress for church, one cannot help wondering what he'd say if he saw an American congregation on Sunday morning—and particularly on Easter.

The most valuable parts of 1 Timothy are the qualifications for bishops and ministers (called deacons) which are spelled out in chapter 3. This ancient counsel is still read at ordination services and at the consecration of bishops, and it is still very sound:

> Now a bishop must be above reproach, married only once, temperate, sensible, dignified, hospitable, an apt teacher, no drunkard, not violent but gentle, not quarrelsome, and no lover of money. He must manage his own household well, keeping his children submissive and respectful in every way, for if a man does not know how to manage his own household, how can he care for God's church? He must not be a recent convert, or he may be puffed up with conceit and fall into the condemnation of the devil; moreover he must be well thought of by outsiders, or he may fall into reproach and the snare of the devil.
>
> 1 Timothy 3:2–7

Also note 1 Timothy 4:1–5, which is a vigorous refutation of the perennially recurring notion that Christianity is an ascetic religion intent upon interfering with man's pleasures. "For everything created by God is good, and nothing is to be rejected if it is received with thanksgiving," says the writer. This passage was cited, among others, in the report of a special commission of the

---

* The verse in question says: "Let a woman learn in silence with all submissiveness."

Episcopal Church upholding temperate use of alcoholic beverages.

Also noteworthy is the advice to the rich, bearing in mind that most of us in modern America are fantastically "rich" by the standards of the first century:

> As for the rich in this world, charge them not to be haughty, nor to set their hopes on uncertain riches but on God who richly furnishes us with everything to enjoy. They are to do good, to be rich in good deeds, liberal and generous, thus laying up for themselves a good foundation for the future, so that they may take hold of the life which is life indeed.
>
> 1 Timothy 6:17–19

Second Timothy is a keep-your-chin-up pep talk from an old preacher to a young one. The emphasis is on endurance, on seeing it through however rough the going becomes. The advice, like so much of Paul's counsel, is still relevant, not only to clergymen but to all who profess to be Christians.

"Take your share of suffering as a good soldier of Jesus Christ," he says, and we listen because we know that he gladly accepted far more than his share.

Some of the best-known passages are 2 Timothy 2:15, 23; and 4:7–8:

> Do your best to present yourself to God as one approved, a workman who has no need to be ashamed, rightly handling the word of truth. . . . Have nothing to do with stupid, senseless controversies; you know that they breed quarrels. . . . I have fought the good fight, I have finished the race, I have kept the faith. Henceforth there is laid up for me the crown of righteousness, which the Lord, the

righteous judge, will award to me on that Day, and
not only to me but also to all who have loved his
appearing.

The third pastoral letter is addressed to TITUS, a
young Gentile from Antioch who accompanied Paul on
some of his missionary travels. Paul thought highly of
Titus, and twice entrusted him with the role of envoy to
the troublesome church at Corinth. Titus later became
the first Christian bishop of Crete.

The brief letter reiterates some of the advice given in
1 Timothy about how a bishop should conduct himself.
There also is an excellent bit of practical wisdom in
Titus 3:9–11 about dealing with inveterate trouble-
makers:

But avoid stupid controversies, genealogies, dissensions, and quarrels over the law, for they are un-
profitable and futile. As for a man who is factious,
after admonishing him once or twice, have nothing
more to do with him, knowing that such a person
is perverted and sinful; he is self-condemned.

THE LETTER TO THE HEBREWS

This is the mystery book of the New Testament. One
of the early church fathers, Origen, said in A.D. 225, that
"God alone knows who wrote the LETTER TO THE HE-
BREWS." Modern scholarship can only say amen to that
verdict. The King James Version calls it a letter of Paul,
but there is almost universal agreement today that, whoever the unknown author may have been, it certainly was
not Paul. The literary style, the figures of speech, the
thought forms, the way of presenting an argument—
nearly everything about the letter is different from the

letters of Paul. Moreover, all of Paul's letters open with a plain declaration of their authorship. But this letter contains no identification of the writer. Despite Origen's pessimism about ever reaching a firm conclusion, scholars have speculated for centuries about various people who *might* have written it. The favored candidate is Barnabas, Paul's early partner in missionary travel. Martin Luther suggested that the author of Hebrews may have been Apollos, whose role in the early Church is described in Acts 18:24–28, and who is mentioned in Paul's first letter to the Corinthians (see page 80 above).

Other nominees include Silas, another missionary companion of Paul's; the apostle Philip; and our old friend Luke. If you want to back a dark horse, a few authorities suspect that Hebrews may have come from the pen of a woman—Priscilla, wife of Aquila, who served under Paul as a teacher in Corinth and Ephesus. Paul's admiration for Priscilla is evident in several of his letters, and considering his general attitude toward female members of the human race, we can safely conclude that she must have been quite a woman.

If we cannot establish the author's name, we can deduce a good many things about him (using the pronoun in the most neutral sense, without prejudice to Priscilla's claims). He was a highly educated person, who wrote excellent Greek (perhaps the purest Greek in the New Testament), and who was conversant with the philosophical ideas of Plato, Aristotle, and Epicurus, to all of which he alludes indirectly but unmistakably. He also knew a great deal about the Old Testament, and was steeped in the attitudes and viewpoints of Judaism.

The destination and date of the letter are also clouded in uncertainty. From internal evidence, we can tell that it was written to a community of Jewish Christians who were undergoing severe persecution. Some think the letter may have been addressed to the church in Jerusalem shortly before the great Roman purge of A.D. 70, which resulted in destruction of the Temple. Others incline to the view that it was written to a Jewish Christian community in Rome during the persecution of Christians undertaken by the Emperor Domitian from 81 to 96.

The writer's purpose is to buck up the Jewish Christians—to keep them from relapsing, under persecution, into the less dangerous faith of Judaism. He recalls the sufferings of Christ, and pleads with his readers to emulate the Lord's steadfastness and courage in meeting danger. His exhortations are accompanied by blunt warnings against apostasy. Having once been brought into the Way, the Truth, and the Life, he asks, "How shall we escape (God's wrath) if we neglect so great a salvation?"

His method is to show, through copious quotations from the Old Testament and an allegorical method of interpretation, that Christ is the fulfillment of the Jewish religion—"the Great High Priest" whose self-sacrifice was a full, perfect, and sufficient satisfaction for the sins of all men in all ages.

The first ten chapters of Hebrews are rather difficult for the modern reader, who does not share the preconceptions and thought forms of Old Testament Judaism. But the eleventh chapter spans the centuries with a high-voltage impact. It is a dissertation on faith, comparable in brilliance and insight to Paul's dissertation on love in 1 Corinthians 13. The sixth verse, in particular, should be pondered most earnestly by any theologian who, having never personally experienced the reality of God, feels impelled to proclaim his "death":

And without faith it is impossible to please him. For whoever would draw near to God must believe that he exists and that he rewards those who seek him.

Hebrews 11:6

Chapter 12 likens Christian living to running a race. It is a counsel of self-discipline and endurance, urgently needed by a church under persecution, and hardly less relevant to a church threatened only by the temptations of an affluent and complacent society.

The final chapter, 13, contains a number of pithy admonitions about hospitality and marital fidelity, and contains in verse 5 a piece of advice that would put television advertisers out of business if modern Christians took it to heart: "Keep your life free from love of money, and be content with what you have; for he has said, 'I will never fail you nor forsake you'" (Hebrews 13:5).

THE GOSPEL ACCORDING TO MATTHEW

In working your way through Paul's letters, you've had a fairly heavy dose of theology *about* Jesus and his significance. Now, as an antidote, go back to the GOSPEL ACCORDING TO MATTHEW and renew your acquaintance with Jesus himself. This is a good rule to follow not only in your first reading of the New Testament, but throughout life. When you feel confused or put off by the doctrines and dogmas and other verbal formulae in which theology has sought to capture the meaning of Christ, the best cure is to discover afresh, in the gospels, the warm, compassionate, tremendously real person whose impact on men and history gave rise to the doctrines.

Matthew's gospel, which is the first book in the New Testament, is traditionally attributed to the apostle Matthew, who first appears in the gospels (see Luke 5:27–29) as Levi, the tax collector. He had been despised by his fellow Jews for collecting taxes for the Roman oppressor, and when he was invited by Jesus to become a member of his inner circle of disciples, he almost fainted from surprise. Matthew's intense gratitude at being accepted still radiates from the 2000-year-old anecdote recorded by Luke.

THE SCHOLARLY ARGUMENT

Whether the apostle Matthew actually wrote the gospel which bears his name is open to question, and the scholarly arguments on the issue provide a good illustration of the methods employed in modern Biblical criticism.

By painstaking comparison of the three synoptic gospels —Matthew, Mark, and Luke—scholars have established, to the satisfaction of all but a few dissenters, that Mark's gospel was written first, and that it was later used as a source and outline by both Luke and the author of Matthew. The gospels of Luke and Matthew duplicate everything that is found in Mark. But they don't stop there. Both Luke and Matthew use a large number of sayings of Jesus, which are so similar in the two gospels as to warrant the conclusion that they were drawn from a common source. This collection of Jesus' teachings, which may well have been the first written document of the Christian Church, is now lost. Scholars refer to it as "Q" from the German word, *Quelle*, which simply means source.

In addition to Mark and "Q," Luke had a good deal of information which he had gathered for himself, by inter-

viewing the Virgin Mary and others (see pages 41–42).
The author of Matthew also had special sources of his
own, which were not available to either Mark or Luke.
For example, only in this gospel do we find the story of
the Wise Men, the flight into Egypt, the conversation in
which Jesus singled out Peter as "keeper of the keys," the
suicide of Judas, and a number of details of the Crucifixion and Resurrection. "Matthew" also is exclusive with
several parables, which we'll identify later in discussing
highlights of the gospel.

Many scholars reason that if Matthew wrote the gospel, he would not have depended so heavily on Mark for
the basic outline of Christ's ministry. After all, Matthew
was there himself, and didn't need to rely on secondhand
sources. Therefore, these scholars assume that what Matthew provided was a collection of Jesus' sayings (perhaps
the "Q" document, perhaps the special material found
only in this gospel) which was incorporated by an unknown author in the book we call Matthew. This theory
postulates that the real author was a non-Palestinian Jew
—probably a citizen of Antioch—who wrote the gospel
about A.D. 90, or even later. Some support for this theory
is found in the writings of the second-century church
father, Papias, who refers to Matthew's having made a
collection of *logia*, or sayings of Christ.

However, there is a flaw in this whole argument that is
perhaps more apparent to a writer than it would be to an
erudite Biblical scholar. I cannot go along with the assumption that Matthew would have found it unnecessary
to use a previously written gospel as a guide to his own
book. On the contrary, if he were writing years after the
events described, it seems to me altogether likely that he
would have gladly made use of whatever outline of the
facts he could find, correcting them wherever they con-

flicted with his own recollection, and adding to them as he could. What is to me most striking is not Matthew's dependence on Mark, but the frequency with which he "corrects" or amplifies Mark's version of an event. The changes often are slight, but they seem to be made with the confidence of an eyewitness.

For this reason, I'm inclined to side with the minority of Biblical scholars who think that the author really was Matthew, and that the book was written about A.D. 70.

THE CHARACTER OF MATTHEW

Whoever the author may have been, all critics would agree with the verdict of Frederick C. Grant that he was "a first-rate literary artist and teacher, who has reflected long and deeply upon the substance of the Christian gospel—both Jesus' life and his teaching—and has combined the teaching material with the biographical narratives in a most appropriate way."

Matthew is sometimes called the most Jewish of the four gospels. Its author was very familiar with the traditions and Scriptures of Judaism (he uses no fewer than sixty quotations from the Old Testament), and he is intent on showing that Jesus was the Messiah of Old Testament prophecy. One of the most distinctive notes of Matthew's gospel is the tendency to digress, after describing something that Jesus did, to show how this fulfilled a particular prophecy.

Another striking characteristic which you will be sure to notice is Matthew's strong attraction to "apocalyptic" writing—speculations about the end of the world. This tendency is prominent in much of the Jewish literature of that period, and it may help you in reading these passages (for example, Matthew 13:24–30, 20:1–16, and

22:1–14) if you bear in mind that the people of Matthew's day were as familiar with this literary genre as you are with the language of advertisements, and they took for granted that the vivid descriptions of "last things" were to be read as poetic imagery rather than as literal forecasts.

THE SERMON ON THE MOUNT

The *pièce de résistance* of Matthew's gospel is the Sermon on the Mount. It takes up three whole chapters—Matthew 5, 6, and 7. In these chapters, Matthew has brought together, through the literary device of a sermon, a priceless collection of Jesus' sayings. Nowhere else in the Bible—indeed, nowhere in the world—will you find such a concentration of sublime ethical teaching. It is impossible to list here all of the gems in this treasure trove: whole books have been written on the Sermon on the Mount, and they do not begin to exhaust its riches. Read it slowly, thoughtfully, and receptively. It will at many points sharply contradict what you may regard as common sense, and demand things which you may think to be impossibly contrary to human nature. That is simply a measure of the radical difference between the way of Christ and the way of the world. While I would not for anything blunt the force of these contradictions or minimize the very great challenge which the Sermon on the Mount makes to our conventional moralities, I would caution you against reading any of Jesus' sayings in a narrowly legalistic or literalistic way. Like all teachers of his time, he frequently used hyperbole to dramatize and drive home his points. When he advises the plucking out of an eye under certain circumstances, he does not really mean that one should blind himself: he is simply underscoring with a vivid metaphor the enormous moral seriousness of lust.

The process of toning down some of Jesus' sayings in the Sermon on the Mount began very early in the Church's history, and you can see evidence of it in Matthew 5:32, where Matthew himself, or some later scribe, has inserted a qualifying clause in Jesus' statement about divorce. The qualification is not found in Mark's version of the saying, and does not sound like Jesus.

Mark's version of what Jesus said is:

> Whoever divorces his wife and marries another, commits adultery against her; and if she divorces her husband and marries another, she commits adultery.

Matthew changes the quotation as follows:

> Everyone who divorces his wife, *except on the ground of unchastity,* makes her an adulteress; and whoever marries a divorced woman commits adultery.

The italicized words indicate the loophole.

Another place in which scholars suspect some doctoring of the original text is Matthew's version of the Lord's Prayer (Matthew 6:5–13). Some manuscripts (including those used in translation of the King James Version) include a doxology, "For thine is the kingdom, the power, and the glory, forever, and ever. Amen." But this is not found in the more ancient manuscripts which have come to light in recent years, and the Revised Standard Version translators reduced the doxology to a footnote. It is noteworthy that the Roman Catholic Church has never acknowledged that the doxology was part of the original prayer which Jesus taught his disciples: that is why, in Catholic worship even today, the "Our Father" ends with what seems to a Protestant jarring suddenness after the final petition, "Deliver us from evil."

No one should be disturbed by the discovery that the doxology is probably a later addition. It merely signifies that the Lord's Prayer had become a staple of Christian worship by the time this gospel was written, and that it was usually followed by a classic Old Testament doxology praising God to whom the prayer was directed. Some scribe felt that it would make things simpler for worshipers if he included the customary doxology right in the text of the prayer.

The remarkable thing about the Bible is not that scholars have found "glosses" or textual changes by scribes, but rather that a century of rigorous investigation has uncovered comparatively few of them—and none which has any important effect on doctrine. Considering all of the hands it has passed through and all of the times it has been recopied for transmission, the Bible has undergone startlingly little textual revision.

OTHER GEMS

One of the gems of Matthew's gospel—particularly helpful to read when you're tired and discouraged—is Jesus' invitation to the careworn:

Come to me, all who labor and are heavy-laden, and I will give you rest.

Take my yoke upon you, and learn from me; for I am gentle and lowly in heart, and you will find rest for your souls.

For my yoke is easy, and my burden is light.
                                        Matthew 11:28–30

Another great passage is the parable of the Last Judgment, in which Jesus seems to say that the one thing that

will really count when we face God is how we've responded to the ordinary human needs of our brothers here
on earth.

When the Son of man comes in his glory, and all the
angels with him, then he will sit on his glorious
throne. Before him will be gathered all the nations,
and he will separate them one from another as a
shepherd separates the sheep from the goats, and he
will place the sheep at his right hand, but the goats at
the left. Then the King will say to those at his right
hand, "Come, O blessed of my Father, inherit the
kingdom prepared for you from the foundation of the
world; for I was hungry and you gave me food, I
was thirsty and you gave me drink, I was a stranger
and you welcomed me, I was naked and you clothed
me, I was sick and you visited me, I was in prison
and you came to me." Then the righteous will answer
him, "Lord, when did we see thee hungry and feed
thee, or thirsty and give thee drink? And when did
we see thee a stranger and welcome thee, or naked
and clothe thee? And when did we see thee sick or
in prison and visit thee?" And the King will answer
them, "Truly, I say to you, as you did it to one of the
least of these my brethren, you did it to me." Then he
will say to those at his left hand, "Depart from me,
you cursed, into the eternal fire prepared for the devil
and his angels; for I was hungry and you gave me no
food, I was thirsty and you gave me no drink, I was
a stranger and you did not welcome me, naked and
you did not clothe me, sick and in prison and you did
not visit me." Then they also will answer, "Lord,
when did we see thee hungry or thirsty or a stranger
or naked or sick or in prison, and did not minister

to thee?" Then he will answer them, "Truly, I say to you, as you did it not to one of the least of these, you did it not to me." And they will go away into eternal punishment, but the righteous into eternal life.

Matthew 25:31–46

Here are some other highlights of Matthew's gospel which are not duplicated elsewhere:

The parable of the sower—Mark has it, too, but much less fully (Matthew 13:1–23). Also see the parables of the Kingdom of God later in the same chapter.

The parable of the unmerciful servant (Matthew 18:23–35).

The parable of the laborers in the vineyard (Matthew 20:1–16).

The parable of the two sons (Matthew 21:28–32).

The parable of the wise and foolish virgins (Matthew 25:1–13).

THE GOSPEL ACCORDING TO MARK

I recommend that you pass over MARK for the present, saving it to be read later when you're partway through the Old Testament. This is in line with the thought voiced earlier that it is helpful to keep coming back to the gospels.

One reason for postponing Mark is that if you read it now, you'll find it dull and repetitious. Every single incident and teaching that Mark records is also reported in one or more of the other gospels, which you've already read. So let's save it for a refresher. But this is a convenient place to discuss its authorship and special characteristics.

As previously stated, Mark is almost universally regarded as the earliest of the four gospels. Most scholars believe it was written in Rome about A.D. 68 by John Mark. Mark is mentioned several times in the Book of Acts. He was the son of one of the first Christian families, and it may have been in his home that Jesus celebrated the Last Supper. He was a companion of Barnabas on missionary journeys, and wound up in Rome as a trusted aide of the aging and soon-to-be-martyred Apostle Peter. In 1 Peter 5:13, the Prince of Apostles refers to him affectionately as "my son Mark."

It is so probable as to be virtually certain that Mark's gospel is based primarily on Peter's firsthand memories of what Jesus said and did. "It is in a sense the Gospel according to Peter," says New Testament scholar Thomas Linton Leishman.

The gospel even shares Peter's well-known predilection for action rather than meditative thought. The narrative moves along at a fast pace. "Immediately" is Mark's favorite word: he uses it forty times in his sixteen brief chapters.

One of the subtler and more touching evidences of Peter's role as the principal source of Mark's information is the fact that Peter appears in this gospel in a much more unfavorable light than he does in the other gospels. The old apostle was quite harsh on himself in recalling years later how he went to sleep during Jesus' agony in the Garden of Gethsemane (Mark 14:37) and how he denied his Lord at the hour of his trial (Mark 14:66–72).

This gospel was written at a time when Christians were undergoing persecution by the mad Roman Emperor Nero. You will see its historical background reflected in Mark's emphasis on Jesus' courage in the face of danger. Another hallmark of Mark's gospel is its stress on Jesus' kindness and unfailing readiness to help anyone in trouble.

THE LETTER OF JAMES

Having read the Sermon on the Mount in Matthew's gospel, let's move now to the LETTER OF JAMES, in which the ethical teaching of the Sermon is reflected more clearly than anywhere else in the New Testament. Martin Luther, who was as testy as Paul about his likes and dislikes, scornfully dismissed James as "an epistle of straw." But his prejudice was based on the mistaken assumption that James disputed Paul's teaching of justification by faith. Actually, as you will see for yourself, there is no real disagreement between James and Paul. James does not minimize the importance of faith, nor does he suggest that salvation can be earned through good works. James simply makes the point that faith in Christ, if genuine, always results in deeds of kindness and mercy toward others.

"Show me your faith apart from your works," he says, "and I by my works will show you my faith."

As Jesus did in the parable of the Last Judgment (Matthew 25:31-46), James emphasizes that the true test of Christian discipleship is how we respond to the practical needs of our fellow men.

"If a brother or sister is ill-clad and in lack of daily food, and one of you says to them, 'Go in peace, be warmed and filled,' without giving them the things needed for the body, what does it profit?" he demanded (James 2:15-16).

The stress on Christianity as a way of life rather than just a set of doctrines is found throughout the letter. James' theme is summed up in one famous sentence: "Be doers of the word, and not hearers only" (James 2:22).

As you may have gathered by this time, I am particularly fond of this book, and can hardly resist quoting it endlessly. But I will leave you the joy of discovering its pearls for yourself.

Among the things you'll want to note particularly are:

The sharp strictures against rich people, and those who toady to them (James 2:1–7, 5:1–6).

The magnificent discourse on the unruliness of the human tongue, and the terrible damage it can do (James 3:2–12).

His thumbnail summary of true religion (James 1:27).

A warning to would-be teachers, and people who write books about the Bible (James 3:1).

A charter for the spiritual healing ministry which is now being revived in many Christian churches (James 5:13–16).

In literary style, James' letter resembles the "wisdom books" of the Old Testament, which we'll be coming to soon. James never beats around the bush. He gets right to the point. In the one hundred and eight verses of his brief letter, there are fifty-four imperatives!

The author identifies himself in the opening verse as "James, a servant of God and of the Lord Jesus Christ."

Most scholars are inclined to accept the traditional view that the James who wrote this letter was "James the Just," the brother or stepbrother of Jesus, who became the head of the church in Jerusalem and one of the most influential figures in the early decades of Christianity. The letter is addressed to "the twelve tribes in the dispersion," which is a metaphor for Jewish Christians scattered through many communities outside Palestine. It probably was written about A.D. 50.

THE FIRST LETTER OF PETER

This is the only surviving document of the New Testament which can confidently be described as having been written by Peter. Although Peter was doubtless the principal source of Mark's gospel, no one has ever suggested that he actually wrote it. But this letter was dictated by Peter to a Greek scribe named Silvanus about A.D. 64, shortly after the outbreak of Nero's persecution of Christians. It apparently was written from Rome, where Peter is believed to have been executed by crucifixion about 65.

Living literally in the shadow of the cross, the old fisherman writes to encourage other Christians who are undergoing what he calls a "fiery trial" by persecution. The faith, courage, and serenity which radiate from this short letter have never been surpassed in any scripture. Benjamin W. Robinson of Chicago Theological Seminary calls it "one of the world's greatest expressions of the glory of fortitude in enduring the hardships of life."

The best testimonial to 1 Peter, however, is that it accomplished its purpose. The little Christian communities did *not* collapse under the ruthless onslaught of the Roman Empire at its cruelest. It is not far-fetched to say that we may owe our own knowledge of Christ to the stiffening of the early Church's backbone which was achieved by apostles like Peter and Paul in letters like this.

Although church members are no longer exposed to any kind of persecution—quite the contrary—Peter's letter has not become merely an antiquarian curiosity. It still speaks to human hearts. It is a fine thing to read when the going gets tough.

Peter does not treat suffering as something which must be endured with stoic resignation. He offers the strange and startling advice that we should continue amidst great suffering to "rejoice with unutterable and exalted joy." These trials are nothing compared to the glory that awaits us as sons of God and joint heirs with Christ. "Therefore gird up your minds." Instead of bemoaning your trials, accept them as an experience that can purify your faith and ennoble your spirit. To suffer when you have done no wrong, to accept pain which you did nothing to deserve, is to emulate Christ by whose wounds we all are healed.

But let us be sure, the apostle cautions, that we really are innocent, and that we suffer for Christ's sake and not because of our own wrongdoing. "Let none of you suffer as a murderer, or a thief, or a wrongdoer, or a mischief-maker."

Peter believed, as did Paul, that the second coming of Christ was imminent.

"The end of all things is at hand," he predicted. "Therefore keep sane and sober for your prayers. Above all, hold unfailingly to your love for one another, for love covers a multitude of sins."

Even though the end did not come as soon as Peter expected, his advice on how to live in a world whose tomorrows are uncertain is still relevant in our nuclear age.

THE SECOND LETTER OF PETER

SECOND PETER purports to have been written by Peter also, but even in the very early years of the Church, there was widespread doubt that it actually came from the apostle. Today nearly all Biblical authorities believe that it was written long after Peter's death by a second-century disciple. The date is variously estimated at A.D. 125 to 150, but in either case it would be the latest docu-

ment included in the New Testament canon. One proof
of its late date is the fact that the author alludes (2 Peter
3:15) to the letters of Paul, in a way that indicates they
had already achieved the status of "scriptures," which certainly was not true in Peter's lifetime. Bruce M. Metzger
points out that "in antiquity, pseudonymous authorship
was a widely accepted literary convention. Therefore, the
use of an apostle's name in reasserting his teaching was
not regarded as dishonest, but merely a way of remind-
ing the Church of what it had received from God through
that apostle."

The author of 2 Peter was deeply concerned about
"false teachers" who were spreading "destructive heresies" including a denial of the lordship of Christ. These
false teachers also were distorting the doctrine of Christian freedom into a license for all kinds of vice. They had
"eyes full of adultery, insatiable for sin." The description
seems to fit what we know of the Gnostic heresy which
swept through many parts of the Church in the second
century.

In addition to warning the flock against these evil doctrines, 2 Peter touches on what must have been a grave
problem for the second-century Church. Christ had not
returned, as the men of the apostolic age had expected
him to do, and "scoffers" were beginning to say that his
second coming was just an illusion. The author of 2 Peter
replies to this attack by saying that God does not measure
time as men do. If the day of judgment has been delayed,
it is only because God is "forbearing" with sinful men,
giving them more time to repent:

> But do not ignore this one fact, beloved, that with
> the Lord one day is as a thousand years, and a thou-
> sand years as one day. The Lord is not slow about

his promise as some count slowness, but is forbearing toward you, not wishing that any should perish, but that all should reach repentance. But the day of the Lord will come like a thief, and then the heavens will pass away with a loud noise, and the elements, will be dissolved with fire, and the earth and the works that are upon it will be burned up.

2 Peter 3:8–10

THE LETTER OF JUDE

JUDE is very brief, a single chapter. It is strikingly similar in content and even in language to 2 Peter, and it seems probable that some borrowing has taken place, one way or the other.

Its author may have been the Jude who is mentioned in the New Testament as a brother or stepbrother of Jesus. There is ancient tradition behind this supposition, and it is further strengthened by the author's description of himself, in the opening verse, as a brother of James. However, the name Jude was quite common in first-century Palestine and it is hard to arrive at definite conclusions about the author's identity. The letter is a so-called "catholic epistle"—that is, one addressed to the Church at large rather than to any particular congregation or group of congregations. It probably was written around A.D. 80.

Since you've already read most of what Jude has to say in 2 Peter, you won't find much noteworthy in this little letter except the conclusion. Verses 24 and 25 contain one of the most beautiful of all benedictions, and if it sounds familiar to you, that's because it is still used every Sunday in thousands of churches.

Now to him who is able to keep you from falling and to present you without blemish before the pres-

ence of his glory with rejoicing, to the only God, our
Savior through Jesus Christ our Lord, be glory, majesty, dominion, and authority, before all time and
now and forever. Amen.

Jude 24-25

REVELATION

This book appears last in the New Testament, and I
will unhesitatingly voice the personal opinion that it is also
least—in terms of what it has to offer the modern reader.
I don't mean that there isn't any spiritual nourishment to
be found in REVELATION. There is. But it is so deeply
embedded in apocalyptic imagery, allegorical symbolism,
and mysticism that you cannot dig it out without the con-
tinual aid of a commentary. And even then, you are apt
to find yourself getting very confused and bewildered.

Worse, some readers make the horrendous mistake of
reading this book literally as a description of heaven and
a detailed forecast of what will happen in the last days.

You will get no quarrel from me if you decide to pass
lightly over this book. But I do recommend that you read
some of it, if only to get the flavor of the apocalyptic
literature which was so popular in the first century.

Another reason for getting acquainted with Revelation
is that you will find in its pages the source of many images
which have become part of our folklore (and which play
a particularly vivid role in Negro spirituals). The pearly
gates, the streets of gold, the Four Horsemen of the
Apocalypse, the battle of Armageddon—all these and
many more come from Revelation.

The book has the same basic purpose as 1 Peter: to encourage Christians undergoing persecution. It was written
around A.D. 90, at the height of the bloody persecution

conducted by the Roman Emperor Domitian. The author was a man named John who had been sent to the island of Patmos, where Christians were exiled for penal servitude in the quarries. Some think that the John who wrote Revelation was the apostle. But this is hard to credit, since his literary style differs quite markedly from that of the Fourth Gospel and the Letters of John. Also, it seems likely that if the author had been the apostle, he would have claimed apostolic status, which meant a lot to his readers. And this he does not do. So the best guess is that this was another John, otherwise unknown to us.

In accordance with the accepted conventions of apocalyptic writing, he cast his message in the form of a series of visions. The basic theme is expressed in Revelation 19:6: "The Lord God Omnipotent reigns." The author is assuring Christians under persecution that God is still master of the universe, and that He will ultimately triumph utterly over evil and open the gates of Paradise to those who have remained steadfast under suffering.

In his book *The Holy Scriptures*, Robert C. Dentan acknowledges that the imagery of Revelation is "strange and often repellent" to the modern reader. But he adds:

"One can read the book with profit and interest if he will only remember that the author . . . is really writing poetry, not prose, and under all the confused images of his supernatural drama is trying to make vivid to his readers the one great truth that all history, both human and cosmic, is under the dominion of Almighty God, so that those who trust and obey Him need have no fear however dark the human situation may seem to be."

IV

READING IN THE OLD TESTAMENT

The reading plan for the New Testament outlined in the preceding chapter was designed to cover virtually all of its contents, on a book-by-book basis.

Now we turn to the Old Testament. And here a different approach is in order. Essentially, it will be a matter of reading *in* the Old Testament,* rather than reading *through* it. We'll skip the genealogies, the repetitive chronicles of Israel's minor kings and their endless wars, and other relatively barren stretches which would put an unduly heavy strain on your resolve to read the Bible.

* And in the Apocrypha, which will be treated as part of the Old Testament.

Also, except in a few instances, we will not be primarily interested in books as a unit of study. Instead, we'll focus on *people* and *events*. One story may take up only part of a book, while another (e.g., the story of Moses) may continue through several books.

Questions of date and authorship, which are sufficiently complicated for the books of the New Testament, become so difficult in the Old Testament that they are best left to scholars. The ordinary reader can settle for the knowledge that the Old Testament is the written distillation of the ancient traditions of a special nation of people who were "called out" by God from all the nomadic tribes of antiquity to be witnesses of His self-revelation and light-bearers to mankind.

In most cases, the books of the Old Testament are not the work of individual writers, but a product of "collective authorship." In their present form, they represent a combining of several original source materials, with the comments and additions of at least one and often a succession of editors.

The first five books of the Old Testament, known as the *Pentateuch* or *Torah,* are a good example of the process of collective authorship. They are traditionally described as "the books of Moses" but, as E. A. Speiser of the University of Pennsylvania points out, "there is no warrant in the Pentateuch itself for ascribing the authorship of the work as a whole to Moses." Most scholars today accept the thesis—one of the first fruits of modern textual criticism—that four different documents have been woven together in the Pentateuch. One of these documents is known as "J" because the author refers to God by the Hebrew proper noun which is customarily translated into English as "Jehovah." Another is called "E" because its author refers to God as "Elohim," the generic Hebrew term for divinity. A third is called "P" because its author is very concerned about the duties and prerogatives of priests. His "signature" is a tendency to refer to God as "El Shaddai"—The Almighty. Finally, a fourth strand, obviously much later and distinctively different from the other three, is called "D" because it is predominant in the book of Deuteronomy.

In the introduction to his magnificent Anchor Bible translation of Genesis, Speiser points out that the recognition of multiple authorship does not "undermine the credibility of the Bible, as has often been feared and alleged." On the contrary, modern scholarship "helps to increase one's respect for the received material beyond the fondest expectations of the confirmed traditionalists." It is now clear, he says, that the Biblical writers faithfully retain details of oral tradition as they had been handed down, even when they seemed to put the founding fathers of the nation in a bad light. For example, Genesis records that Abraham and his son, on visits to foreign lands, spoke of their wives as their sisters. Their reasons for doing this had been forgotten for centuries at the time the written record was made, but the writer preserved the fact as it had been transmitted, attributing it to the only motive he could think of: cowardice. Modern research has disclosed that in the Hurrian society from which Abraham came, a wife acquired special dignity and protection if her husband designated her publicly as his sister. Wives were a dime a dozen in that polygamistic society, but a man's sister had to be treated with the same courtesy that was due to him. So Abraham was being gallant, not craven, when he called his wife his sister. But the author of the story in Genesis did not realize this, and the fact that he recorded the detail anyway gives us grounds for confidence in the care with which ancient tradition was preserved in the writing of the Bible. At the same time, the fact that the writer felt free to inject his own erroneous explanation alerts us to the human element in the Scriptures, and reminds us to beware, particularly in the Old Testament, of the kind of narrow Biblical literalism that regards every sentence of the ancient text as having been dictated by God.

You will see as you read in the Old Testament that it contains a greater variety of literary forms than the New Testament. History and myth, prose and poetry, biography and legend are closely interwoven and it is not always easy to tell where one leaves off and the other begins. This need not cause you any great difficulty, if you bear in mind what was said in Chapter II about reading Biblical stories for their *religious* significance. To quote Speiser once again, the Old Testament "is ultimately the story of the gradual evolution of the monotheistic ideal.

"That ideal was first glimpsed and pursued by a single society in resolute opposition to prevailing beliefs. In the course of that quest, certain truths emerged which proved to possess universal validity. . . . Hence the abiding appeal of the Bible, which is the comprehensive record of that quest."

"IN THE BEGINNING . . ."

The first eleven chapters of the BOOK OF GENESIS are devoted to prehistoric myths about the creation of the universe, the origin of species, the advent of man, and his early affinity for evil ways. The authors of Genesis had no idea of encompassing all of primeval history—from the dawn of creation to the age of Abraham, about 1800 B.C. —in so brief a space. Their purpose was simply to create a universal setting for the history of the Hebrew people.

These eleven chapters of Genesis have probably caused more popular confusion and controversy than all the rest of the Bible put together. In them you'll find the classic Sunday School stories—Adam and Eve, Noah's ark, the tower of Babel, et al—which are perennial bones of contention between Biblical literalists and skeptics.

It is a pity that all this senseless argument has obscured the real point of these ancient stories. Read for their religious meaning, they are among the noblest passages of the whole Bible.

Consider, for example, the famous first chapter of Genesis, which tells how God created the world in six days. It is quite obviously based on a Mesopotamian creation myth which archaeologists have found on cuneiform tablets written centuries before Genesis. No one should be surprised at this. The Bible records that the founder of the Hebrew nation, Abraham, came originally from Mesopotamia. It was perfectly natural that Abraham should have passed along to his descendants much of the myth and folklore of the culture from which he came.

What is significant about the first chapter of Genesis is not the superficial resemblance it bears to the Mesopotamian creation myth, but rather the tremendous difference which took place in the story when it was retold by the ancient Hebrews. The Mesopotamian version describes the various steps in creation as the work of various rival deities. But the Hebrew version is a majestic affirmation of monotheism. It tells us there is one God who brought the whole universe into being and whose sovereign will is reflected in every detail of His creation. Modern science has given us a far better understanding of the various natural processes—such as evolution—through which this creative will worked. But science has not, will not, and cannot refute the real point of Genesis 1, which is that

God is "the beginning," the ultimate source, the ground of being.

Chapter 1 is from the "P" document and reflects a rather sophisticated stage of Hebrew religious development. Chapters 2 and 3 give a different account of creation, from "J." It is more primitive in its theology, and speaks of God in anthropomorphic terms. It tells the story of Adam and Eve in the Garden of Eden. That this story was understood by the ancient Hebrews as a myth rather than literal history is clear from the name Adam, which is Hebrew for "Everyman." The point of the myth is that man alienates himself from God through stubborn self-will and disobedience. You are not likely to find anywhere in the Bible, or anywhere in contemporary literature, a more profound truth about human nature.

Chapters 6 through 9 contain the story of the Flood. This ancient myth also came originally from Mesopotamia. Many of the details—including the Ark—are found in a collection of tablets known as the Gilgamesh Epic. It is very likely that the story reflects the memory of a real flood which devastated the Mesopotamian valley between the Tigris and Euphrates rivers. Whatever its origin, the story has undergone a striking change in the course of its transmission from Mesopotamian to Hebrew folklore. The Mesopotamian version is simply an adventure yarn about a big flood and a smart fellow (named Utnapishtim) who saw it coming and managed to save himself, his family and his livestock by building a big boat. In Genesis, the story is given a moral point. The Flood is depicted as God's judgment on "the wickedness of man," which had become so bad as to cause God to repent of ever having created human beings. Noah is spared, not by his own heroics, but by the grace of God, with whom he had "found favor" by righteous conduct.

Chapter 11 offers still another Mesopotamian story which has been turned into the vehicle for a Hebrew moral insight. It tells of the building of a high tower. Originally it was just a gee-whiz story of the kind that might have been put out by the Babylon Chamber of Commerce. In Genesis, it becomes a parable about human pride and presumptuousness.

THE PATRIARCHS

The history of the Hebrew people begins in chapter 12 of Genesis, with the story of Abraham.

Abraham was not a mythical figure like Adam and Noah. He was a real person, who lived in Mesopotamia about 1800 B.C. This was the golden age of Babylonian civilization. What we know from independent historical sources about Mesopotamia during the Hammurabi dynasty bears out what the Bible clearly implies: that Abraham was enjoying a good life in his native land and had every reason for wanting to stay put.

But God called him to a different destiny. Genesis 12:1–3 records the command and the promise which Abraham received:

> Go forth from your native land
> And from your father's home
> To a land that I will show you.
> I will make of you a great nation,
> Bless you, and make great your name. . . .

And the next verse records Abraham's response with magnificent simplicity:

"So Abram went, as the Lord had told him . . ."

With his brother Lot and his wife Sarah and all his servants and possessions (which evidently were considerable), Abraham set forth on an epic journey which led

HITTITES

MEDITERRANEAN
SEA

Haran

Tadmor

EUPHRATES RIVER

MESOPOTAMIA

TIGRIS RIVER

Hazor
CANAAN
Mamre
Shechem
Jerusalem

Damascus

ABRAHAM'S

Babylon

ARABIAN

DESERT

JOURNEY

Ur

Memphis

EGYPT

PERSIAN
GULF

RED
SEA

The World of
the Patriarchs

him at last to the Promised Land of Canaan (see map
above). The Bible does not depict Abraham as a man of
outstanding wisdom or heroic courage. His great virtue
was unhesitating obedience to the will of God. His readiness to obey, at whatever cost, is dramatically illustrated
in Genesis 22:1–19, which tells how God tested Abraham's
faithfulness by ordering him to make a sacrifice of his son,
Isaac:

> After these things God tested Abraham, and said
> to him, "Abraham!" And he said, "Here am I." He
> said, "Take your son, your only son Isaac, whom you

love, and go to the land of Moriah, and offer him there as a burnt offering upon one of the mountains of which I shall tell you." So Abraham rose early in the morning, saddled his ass, and took two of his young men with him, and his son Isaac; and he cut the wood for the burnt offering, and arose and went to the place of which God had told him. On the third day Abraham lifted up his eyes and saw the place afar off. Then Abraham said to his young men, "Stay here with the ass; I and the lad will go yonder and worship, and come again to you." And Abraham took the wood of the burnt offering, and laid it on Isaac his son; and he took in his hand the fire and the knife. So they went both of them together. And Isaac said to his father Abraham, "My father!" And he said, "Here am I, my son." He said, "Behold, the fire and the wood; but where is the lamb for a burnt offering?" Abraham said, "God will provide himself the lamb for a burnt offering, my son." So they went both of them together.

When they came to the place of which God had told him, Abraham built an altar there, and laid the wood in order, and bound Isaac his son, and laid him on the altar, upon the wood. Then Abraham put forth his hand, and took the knife to slay his son. But the angel of the Lord called to him from heaven, and said, "Abraham, Abraham!" And he said, "Here am I." He said, "Do not lay your hand on the lad or do anything to him; for now I know that you fear God, seeing you have not withheld your son, your only son, from me." And Abraham lifted up his eyes and looked, and behold, behind him was a ram, caught in a thicket by his horns; and Abraham went and took the ram, and offered it up as a burnt offering instead

of his son. So Abraham called the name of that place
The Lord will provide; as it is said to this day, "On
the mount of the Lord it shall be provided."

And the angel of the Lord called to Abraham a second time from heaven, and said, "By myself I have
sworn, says the Lord, because you have done this,
and have not withheld your son, your only son, I will
indeed bless you, and I will multiply your descendants as the stars of heaven and as the sand which is
on the seashore. And your descendants shall possess
the gate of their enemies, and by your descendants
shall all the nations of the earth bless themselves, because you have obeyed my voice." So Abraham returned to his young men, and they arose and went
together to Beer-sheba; and Abraham dwelt at Beer-
sheba.

Genesis 22:1–19

You will want to read all of the story of Abraham, which
continues through Genesis 25:10. In addition to the poignant story of the "sacrifice" of Isaac, you will find a vivid
and very human account of Abraham's woman troubles,
which culminated in the driving away of his concubine
Hagar and her son Ishmael. It will heighten the interest
of this story if you bear in mind that Islamic lore depicts
Ishmael as the forefather of all Arabic peoples—thus pro-
jecting Arab-Jewish tensions all the way back to Abraham's quarrelsome womenfolk.

Another highlight is the hair-raising tale of the destruction of Sodom, a city whose depravity is commemorated
to this day by the use of the word "sodomy" as a legal
term for homosexual conduct. The fate of Lot's wife is
an early Biblical testimony to the strength of feminine
curiosity.

After Abraham's death at what the Bible calls "the good old age" of 175, his covenant with God passed to his son Isaac. Isaac seems to have been a dependable but rather colorless man. Although the Biblical record abounds with anecdotes about his father Abraham and his son Jacob, there is relatively little of a personal nature about Isaac. He appears mainly as a supporting player in stories that are primarily concerned with either his father or his son.

Even Isaac's wife, Rebekah, who was an early version of the mail-order bride, comes through as a much more vivid personality than her husband. There is only one chapter in the Bible—Genesis 26—which gives Isaac the center of the stage, and it is mainly concerned with his activities as a well-digger.

Jacob—the third generation of the patriarchs—is one of the most colorful characters in the Old Testament. His story begins in chapter 27 with a dastardly act, in which Jacob cunningly cheats his brother Esau out of his birthright. It is noteworthy that no attempt has been made to clean up the story, or to justify Jacob's rascality. The authors of the Bible took human nature as they found it, and even the great heroes, like Jacob, Moses, and David, are candidly drawn, warts and all.

Jacob gets his come-uppance when he returns to the ancestral home in Mesopotamia to find a wife. Here he encounters in his uncle Laban as devious a schemer as himself. There's no better reading in the Old Testament than the story of Jacob's romance with the comely Rachel, and the dirty trick which Laban played on him on his wedding night. You'll find it in Genesis 29. The story of Jacob continues through chapter 36, and is all worth reading. You will learn, among other things, how Jacob's name was changed to Israel, so that his descendants were known as the children of Israel.

Beginning with the thirty-seventh chapter, the story of Genesis is dominated by Joseph and his brothers—the fourth generation of patriarchs. If you skip chapter 38, which is a distracting digression, the story unfolds as a single narrative of great dramatic force. As Hollywood has discovered, the story has everything—fraternal jealousy, hairbreadth escapes, the efforts of a sex-starved wife to lure a handsome young man into her bed, the triumph of virtue, and a schmaltzy reconciliation scene in which Joseph is reunited with the brothers who tried to do him in. It ends in chapter 47 on an upbeat, with Joseph serving as Grand Vizier to the Pharaoh, the most powerful office in Egypt. You can skip the last three chapters of Genesis —48, 49, and 50—which are anticlimactic.

MOSES AND THE EXODUS

The Book of Genesis closes with Jacob's family—"the children of Israel"—comfortably settled in Egypt, whence they had gone to escape from famine in Palestine. With brother Joseph running the kingdom as Grand Vizier, the Israelites enjoyed a privileged position. Genesis 47:27 reports that they settled in the part of Egypt known as the land of Goshen "and they gained possessions in it, and were fruitful and multiplied exceedingly."

The Israelites remained in Egypt for more than 400 years. They evidently had it pretty good until about 1250 B.C., when, we are told in the opening chapter of the BOOK OF EXODUS, "there arose a new king over Egypt" who viewed the unassimilated Semitic tribe as a menace to Egypt's internal security. This forerunner of Adolf Hitler was the Pharaoh Rameses II. He made slaves of the Israelites and drove them to forced labor on public works, such as building pyramids. When they continued to multiply in spite of hardships, he issued orders that all their male babies should be put to death. It was during this period of persecution that a Hebrew woman, identified only as "a daughter of Levi," bore a son. "And when she saw that he was a goodly child, she hid him three months. And when she could hide him no longer, she took for him a basket made of bulrushes, and daubed it with bitumen and pitch; and she put the child in it and placed it among the reeds at the river's brink" (Exodus 2:2–3).

You probably know what happened next: it is perhaps the most familiar of all Sunday School stories. Pharaoh's daughter came down to bathe in the Nile, found the basket, fell in love with its tiny human cargo, and took the baby home to be reared as her own son. She gave him an Egyptian name—*Moses*. He was truly a child of destiny, for he was to lead the Israelites out of bondage in the great trek which is called the Exodus.

The Exodus is one of the watershed events in human history. It transformed a rabble of slaves into a nation of people who were to make an immeasurable contribution to the religious, moral, and cultural heritage of mankind. It is not sufficient to say that the Exodus is the central story of the Old Testament. The fact is, without the Exodus there would have *been* no Old Testament. Instead of becoming the people who produced the Bible, the Hebrews would have disappeared from history, either by gradual extermination in slavery, or by assimilation into Egypt's polyglot population.

As leader of the Exodus and founding father of the Hebrew nation, Moses is one of the authentic great men of history. Even if his stature were measured solely by his political and military accomplishments, he would merit a place with Alexander the Great, Julius Caesar, Napoleon, George Washington, and Winston Churchill in the first rank of men who have exhibited a genius for leadership. But there was another dimension to Moses, which lifts him into even more select company. He was also a great religious leader. In the religion of Judaism, Moses occupies a place comparable to that of Buddha in Buddhism, and Mohammed in Islam. He is scarcely less significant to those of Christian heritage. Of all the thousands of persons whom you'll meet in the Bible, there is only one—Jesus Christ himself—who lived in more intimate communion with God than Moses.

The biography of Moses and the history of the Exodus are must reading for anyone who is even moderately curious about the origins of Western civilization and the Judeo-Christian moral code. Outlined below is a reading plan which will enable you to cover all of the highlights of the story, skipping over passages which are repetitious, relatively unimportant, or filled with tedious details about the design of various items used in Hebrew worship.

THE PARTS YOU SHOULD READ

We will also save for separate reading later a number of long "statutory" passages which give details of the Mosaic law.

You may find it convenient to take your Bible now and mark the chapters you're going to read in following the story of Moses and the Exodus. Some people have a vague feeling of sacrilege about marking up a Bible. This is absurd. The Bible is meant to be read, and one of the signs of a well-read book is that it's full of underscorings, marginal notations and other markings. So, take pen, pencil or crayon (I personally lean toward a ballpoint pen with red ink) and mark off the following passages to be read in order:

Exodus 1:1–20:26
Exodus 32:1–34:35
 Skip the whole book of Leviticus.
Numbers 10:11–27:23
 Numbers 31:1–34:12
Deuteronomy 5:1–8:20
Deuteronomy 29:1–34:12

You will observe that this reading plan begins with one large, solid chunk: the first twenty chapters of Exodus. Here you will find a single continuous narrative which for color and excitement has few peers in world literature. The first four chapters describe the plight of the Israelites and the dramatic confrontation on Mount Horeb in which Moses heard the voice of God commanding him to "bring forth my people" out of captivity. It seems to me irrelevant to the point of blasphemy to argue about whether God literally addressed Moses out of a burning bush, or whether this story is a mythical representation of an inner spiritual experience. The *point* is that God communicated in a vivid and unmistakable way with a man who had hitherto been anything but a religious mystic, and who had never before envisioned himself as the liberator of the Hebrews. Moses' reluctance to take on the job is characteristic of him: like Jesus, he was at once a person of supreme confidence and great humility.

In chapters 5 through 10, we see Moses trying to persuade Pharaoh to heed God's command, "Let my people go!" Pharaoh is stubborn, even though the land is swept by a series of plagues which Moses identifies as warnings of God's displeasure. Bear in mind that the Biblical account of these happenings was written down centuries later, and was based on folk stories handed down verbally through many generations. A certain amount of legendary heightening of the story is to be expected in this kind of transmission. That it has in fact taken place is amply demonstrated by such passages as Exodus 7:22, which says that Pharaoh was not much impressed with Moses' turning the water of the Nile into blood because "the magicians of Egypt did the same by their secret arts." I am prepared to believe that God could change water into blood if He chose to do so, but I repose no such faith in the secret arts of Egyptian magicians.

The account of the plagues builds to a dramatic climax with the story of the first Passover in chapters 11 and 12. More than thirty-two centuries later, Jews throughout the world still keep the commandment laid down in Exodus 12:24 by observing an annual commemoration of the Passover. In reading these chapters, you will learn, among other things, why your Jewish neighbors eat unleavened bread during the Passover celebration.

The dreadful punishment visited on the Egyptians on Passover night broke Pharaoh's resistance—temporarily. "Be gone!" he told Moses. The Israelites left immediately. But Pharaoh, who was a very changeable fellow, repented his decision to release so many valuable slaves. He called out the cavalry and gave hot pursuit.

Chapter 14 of Exodus tells how God delivered the Israelites with a mighty act. He sent a strong wind to divide the waters of a sea which blocked their path, enabling them to pass through on dry land. When Pharaoh's soldiers tried to follow, the sea closed over them and drowned them. The body of water involved in this episode has been identified erroneously in English Bibles for centuries. Even a comparatively recent translation like the Revised Standard Version calls it the Red Sea. But in the last few years, scholars have determined that the most ancient manuscripts of Exodus refer not to the Red Sea, but to "the Sea of Reeds." This was a shallow body of water north of the Red Sea. That a strong wind should create a temporary causeway through such a body of water is by no means a far-fetched idea. But let us beware of too-easy naturalistic explanations. The point of the story of the Exodus is that God intervened in history to deliver a people from captivity. We can believe that he employed natural mechanisms of cause-and-effect—indeed, the Bible explicitly says that He did. But if we go further and attribute to accident or coincidence the timing of the wind which brought the Israelites to safety and their pursuers to watery death, we are in effect denying that God had any hand in the matter. And any such denial would be a display of intellectual arrogance on our part. The eyewitnesses—the people who were *there*—were absolutely certain that something extraordinary had taken place. Their conviction that they had been saved—not by luck, not by their own fortitude, not by any natural circumstance but by a miraculous intervention of God—became the very foundation of the Hebrew religion. It was a conviction so strong that it survived all of their subsequent lapses into faithlessness and apostasy. It was passed down to their children and their children's children as the one sure fact in their history, in light of which all other facts must be judged. If we come along more than 3000 years later and blandly say that they mistook a perfectly normal event for a miracle, we will find ourselves contending that the whole history of Israel is based on a delusion. There may be some people who find this a satisfactory explanation; for myself, I can no more believe it than I can believe that the Christian Church grew out of a mass hallucination, rather than an actual Resurrection.

In chapter 15, we find a song which many scholars regard as the oldest literary form preserved in the Bible.

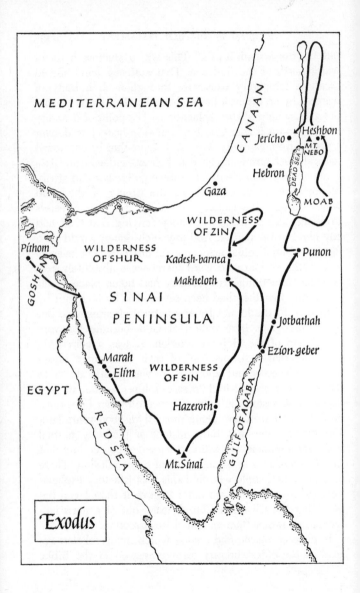

Exodus

Great events in a people's history were celebrated in song long before they were reduced to the kind of prose which we today would call historical narrative. It is easy to believe that this song was sung around the campfires of the Israelites during their long years of wandering in the Sinai desert. It served to bolster their faith in hours of trial, and to remind them of their past in times of ungrateful prosperity. It probably was passed down from generation to generation with little change: songs are easy to memorize, and they do not lend themselves readily to editorial changes. That this particular song should have survived intact is all the more plausible because it has the beauty of great epic poetry:

I will sing to the Lord, for he has triumphed gloriously:
The horse and his rider he has thrown into the sea.
The Lord is my strength and my song,
And he has become my salvation;
This is my God, and I will praise him,
My father's God, and I will exalt him. . . .

Three months after they had fled Egypt, the Israelites reached the foot of Mount Sinai (see map page 136). They pitched camp here, and Moses climbed to the top of the holy mountain to commune with God. When he came down, he brought the Ten Commandments, which you will find in the twentieth chapter of Exodus.

The narrative is interrupted at this point by the insertion of a long list of other rules and regulations which were part of the Mosaic law. We'll return to them later. For now, skip them and pick up at chapter 32 where the narrative resumes. Moses had been on the mountain for forty days and nights, and during his absence, the Israelites had indulged in what the Bible depicts as their incurable national weakness. They lapsed into idolatry, and built themselves a golden calf to worship.

Chapter 32 gives us perhaps our best glimpse into the complex, powerful personality of Moses. First we find him interceding for his people, pleading with God not to destroy them for their apostasy. Then we see him venting his own hot anger upon the wayward children for whom he has prayed. In his wrath, he "took the calf which they had made, and burnt it with fire, and ground it to powder, and scattered it upon the water, and made the people drink it."

THE BOOKS OF NUMBERS AND DEUTERONOMY

From chapter 38 of Exodus, which concludes the episode at Mount Sinai, we skip right over the Book of Leviticus to the tenth chapter of the BOOK OF NUMBERS, where the narrative resumes at the eleventh verse with the Israelites setting out from Mount Sinai. The next seventeen chapters chronicle various adventures of their desert wanderings, and are worth reading although not of crucial importance. One portion which I do most earnestly commend to your attention is the delightful story of the prophet Balaam and his donkey, which begins in chapter 22.

The BOOK OF DEUTERONOMY is cast in the literary form of three long farewell addresses by Moses. It repeats, summarizes, and in some important instances, reinterprets the vast code of Mosaic law which has been given piecemeal in Exodus, Leviticus, and Numbers. The first four chapters are an abbreviated review of the history of Israel, and you can skip them if you've already read the long version in the earlier books. Chapter 5 of Deuteronomy gives a second version of the Ten Commandments. It is almost identical to that in Exodus 20, with one minor but interesting exception. Sabbath observance is treated in Exodus as a duty man owes to God. In the Deuteronomy version, the Sabbath is depicted as a gift of God to man, and its purpose is to insure "that your manservant and maidservant may rest as well as you." The point proved hard to get across, however. More than a millennium later, Jesus had to say all over again that "the sabbath was made for man, not man for the sabbath" (Mark 2:27).

Deuteronomy was evidently one of Jesus' favorite books of Scripture. He often quoted it in his own teachings. In chapter 6 you'll find the famed "Shema" or creed of Judaism—"Hear, O Israel: the Lord our God is one Lord. . . ." And just after it comes the first of the two sentences which Jesus took from different parts of Old Testament and combined to form what we now call the Summary of the Law: "You shall love the Lord your God with all your heart, and with all your soul, and with all your might" (Deuteronomy 6:5). Jesus, quoting this admonition, called it "the first and great commandment." To it he linked another commandment, which is given, without any particular emphasis, is an isolated sentence of Leviticus 19:18: "You shall love your neighbor as yourself." On these two commandments, Jesus said, "hang all the law and the prophets" (Matthew 22:36-40). This is an excellent example of Jesus' attitude toward the Old Testament Scriptures. He knew them intimately, revered them, and quoted from them. But he did not hesitate to be selective, to assign greater value to some portions than to others. Jesus was *not* a Biblical literalist.

In the twenty-ninth through the thirty-fourth chapters of Deuteronomy, we find Moses at the twilight of his long and eventful life, preaching a final sermon to his beloved but "stiff-necked" people, and then climbing alone to the top of a mountain to die. His last act was typical of Moses. He made sure that there would be no tomb of Moses which might become an idolatrous substitute for the worship of the unseen God. Deuteronomy 34 says that God himself buried Moses and "no man knows the place of his burial to this day." The story concludes with a magnificent epitaph:

"And there has not arisen a prophet since in Israel like Moses, whom the Lord knew face to face."

THE MOSAIC LAW

For the sake of continuity, we have passed over, in reading the story of Moses, a number of lengthy passages which spell out the extremely detailed code of moral, sanitary, ritualistic, economic, and criminal legislation which is known as the Mosaic law. It is worth going back to examine at least some of these passages. It is a cardinal point of Christian doctrine—you will remember Paul was always stressing it—that the "new dispensation" in Christ has released his followers from the obligation of obeying the letter of the Mosaic law. On the other hand, it should be borne in mind that Jesus never repealed any of the *moral* precepts of the Mosaic law. When he changed them at all, it was only to make them stiffer—as in the case of his teachings about divorce and adultery. In his own words, Jesus sought "not to destroy but to fulfill" the Mosaic law.

As you read the rules which Moses gave to the Israelites, or which evolved later in their history and were attributed to him, bear in mind the kind of world in which this legislation was formulated. The so-called *lex talionis* which decrees "an eye for an eye and a tooth for a tooth" may sound almost barbaric to a society conditioned (if not entirely persuaded) by twenty centuries of Christian teaching about forgiving your enemies. But it was a very advanced and humane concept in the thirteenth century B.C., because its purpose was not to encourage, but to *limit* revenge. Instead of killing a man who had knocked out one of your teeth, you were limited to knocking out one of his teeth.

Similarly, you will find that the Mosaic law permitted slavery. Instead of being horrified at this fact, however, you may marvel at the effort which the Law makes to ameliorate the ancient institution of slavery and to insure that even slaves had inalienable rights as human beings. This is spelled out in the twenty-first chapter of Exodus, which also includes the *lex talionis.*

Here are some other chapters which contain important segments of the Mosaic code:

Exodus 22—rules governing theft, seduction, witches, sex relations with animals, and lending money on interest.

Exodus 23—rules about perjury, fair treatment of strangers, good agricultural practice (letting the land lie fallow every seventh year), the keeping of feasts, and the cryptic sentence which prevents Orthodox Jews from cooking meat in any utensil which has been used to contain dairy products: "You shall not boil a kid in its mother's milk."

Leviticus 11—the famous dietary laws. Note that they ban not only pork, but also rabbit, camel meat, shellfish such as shrimp and crab, eagles and other birds of prey, certain winged insects (but not grasshoppers and crickets), and rattlesnake steaks.

Leviticus 12—rules regarding circumcision.

Leviticus 13, 14, 15—sanitary regulations dealing with quarantine of lepers and other health problems.

Leviticus 17—rules for kosher slaughter of livestock (designed to insure that no blood is eaten).

Leviticus 19—humanitarian laws about leaving the gleanings of a harvest for the hungry, not bearing grudges, loving your neighbor as yourself, and honoring the elderly.

Deuteronomy 13—stern rules for the suppression of heresy.

Deuteronomy 15—social legislation for protection of the poor.

Deuteronomy 19—criminal law, including the famed law of sanctuary.

Deuteronomy 21—rules on a variety of matters, from how to treat captured womenfolk to the disciplining of rebellious sons.

Deuteronomy 22:5—more miscellaneous laws, dealing with the robbing of birds' nests, bannisters on roofs, the proper planting of vineyards, and how to yoke oxen.

Scattered through Leviticus and Deuteronomy are scores of laws governing sexual conduct. They get right down to cases, and cover every imaginable type of normal and aberrant behavior. You will find some of the more significant sex legislation in the following passages:

> Leviticus 20:10–21
> Leviticus 21:1–9
> Deuteronomy 22:5
> Deuteronomy 22:13–24
> Deuteronomy 24:1–5
> Deuteronomy 25:5–10

Altogether there are 613 specific commandments in the Mosaic code as it is spelled out in the first five books of the Bible. Of these, 365 are "shall nots"—that is, they deal with things that should not be done—while the remaining 248 are positive, "you shall . . ." That the negative commandments outnumber the positive is no reflection on the Mosaic law: lawyers will tell you that the same thing is true of any legal code, including our contemporary U.S. statutes. This simply reflects the fact that it is generally much easier to define types of conduct which are illegal than to stipulate positive acts which must be performed.

What was said earlier will bear repeating: when you read the Mosaic law, do not expect to find in it ethical concepts as sublime as those which you will find in the New Testament, or in the fully developed Judaism of the great prophets.

"The miraculous thing about these (Mosaic) laws," says Frederick C. Grant, "is that, rising out of the morass of ancient Semitic paganism with its superstitious, magic and crude fertility rites, here was a tender shoot sprung from the tiny acorn of religious faith and ethical conviction, destined to grow into a mighty oak and survive the storms of centuries."

The first five books of the Old Testament are traditionally designated books of law (in Hebrew, *Torah*), although, as we have seen, they also contain a great deal of history.

Now we come to another major subdivision of the Old Testament which tells what happened to the Israelites after they ended their long, wandering trek through the desert and settled down to become a nation.

The books of Joshua, Judges, 1 and 2 Samuel, and 1 and 2 Kings are worthy of your attention although—let it be plainly admitted at the outset—they do not represent a high-water mark of Biblical spirituality. You will not often encounter in these books passages which will nourish your soul in the same direct, immediate way as a chapter of the New Testament, a psalm, or the writings of the prophets.

Why, then, should you bother to read this part of the Bible? There are several reasons.

First, it contains an important part of Israel's history with which you must be familiar in order to understand other parts of the Bible, including the New Testament.

Second, it contains some of the most illuminating and entertaining biographies to be found in the Bible or anywhere else in literature. The men and women you will meet in these six books are not all admirable servants of God. Along with heroes and heroines, you will find rascals and hussies. Often—as in the magnificently told story of David—you will see both heroism and rascality united in one complex, dynamic human being.

The anonymous biographers and historians who wrote this part of the Bible sometimes pronounce explicit moral judgments on men and events. They will say that Israel got into trouble because of a particular misdeed, or that a certain leader went wrong because of a specific flaw of character. But the moral lessons you derive from these stories need not always be the ones the author had in mind. Whenever a biographer makes it possible for us to see into another man's life, we can acquire insights into human nature which are applicable to our own problems. So in reading the stories of Joshua, Gideon, Samson, Samuel, Saul, David, Solomon, Elijah, Jezebel, and other fascinating characters who await you in the sixth through the eleventh books of the Old Testament, don't assume the role of a detached spectator. You are reading these stories, not just to gain information about a certain period of ancient history, but to hear what God may have to say to *you* through them. It may take a while before you come to a shoe that fits, but you will assuredly find one, and probably many, if you seek time-transcending parallels between the problems and temptations that confronted men like David in the Jerusalem of 1000 B.C., and those which confront you in twentieth-century America.

THE CONQUEST OF CANAAN

After the death of Moses, the role of leader passed to his chosen successor, Joshua. You will recall having met him earlier—as the Israelite general in the battle against Amalek, (Exodus 17) and as head of the espionage team which Moses sent into Canaan (Numbers 13, 14). His name means "deliverer" in Hebrew; one of its variants is *Jesus*.

Joshua led the Israelites across the Jordan River to conquer and occupy the Promised Land—so called because it was promised by God to Abraham and his descendants (Genesis 12:1–7). The Promised Land, or Canaan as it was known in those days, lay between the Jordan and the Mediterranean, bounded on the north by the Lebanon mountains, and on the south by the Negeb desert (see map on page 147). It came to be known later in history as Palestine. It is now divided into the states of Israel and Jordan.

The Israelite conquest of Canaan is recounted in the sixth book of the Old Testament, which is called JOSHUA in honor of its dominant figure. This is the most sanguinary book in the Bible, and it reflects an extremely primitive view of God as a tribal deity who sternly punishes his own people if they stray from the path of strict obedience, and who is either indifferent or actively hostile toward all other peoples.

The tone of the book is epitomized by Joshua 8:24–25, which records with glee the carnage inflicted upon Israel's enemies in the battle of Ai:

When Israel had finished slaughtering all the inhabitants of Ai in the open wilderness where they pursued them and all of them to the very last had fallen by the edge of the sword, all Israel returned to the city of Ai, and smote it with the edge of the sword. And all who fell that day, both men and women, were twelve thousand, all people of Ai.

This outdoes even a modern communiqué in emphasizing the enemy's losses while minimizing those suffered by one's own side.

Considering our own propensity for believing that God is on our side of all international quarrels, we should be slow to criticize the Israelites for assuming that their conquest of Canaan was a holy war in which the end justified any means. However, we cannot help but reflect that to the Canaanites who found themselves under sudden and violent attack, the invasion must have seemed like an act of naked and unprovoked aggression. And, no matter how often we remind ourselves that we, too, call ourselves "a nation under God," and fully expect His help in our wars, it comes as something of a shock to read in the tenth chapter of Joshua that God made the sun stand still in order to give the Israelites more time in which to carve up a demoralized and fleeing enemy army. And perhaps still more startling is the report, in the same chapter, that God took an active part in the battle, throwing down

The Conquest of Canaan

"great stones from heaven" to bash the heads of the enemy troops.

All right—so you don't believe in a God who throws rocks. Neither do I. This is a good example of what I meant earlier by saying that we must read the Old Testament in the light of the New Testament. It is in Jesus Christ that we see God as He really is, and confidence in that revelation enables us to acknowledge without qualms the inadequacies of an ancient theology.

THE RELEVANCE OF JOSHUA'S STORY

It may seem surprising, at first glance, to encounter in Joshua a far more primitive view of God than we found earlier in the teachings of Moses. Here is plain contradiction of the notion that the Old Testament records a progressive evolution in the Israelite concept of God. Under the pressure of a hard and bloody war, the Israelites retrogressed in their religious insights—even as we are wont to do.

And this is one of the reasons why we can profit from reading the book of Joshua. It is more relevant to our present situation than we may like to admit. For we live in a world not unlike that of Joshua—a world of violence and discord, in which it is terribly easy for God-fearing people to become calloused about wholesale death, indifferent to the sufferings of human beings who have been cast by circumstances in the role of the enemy. In Joshua we see ourselves as we may all too readily become.

There is, of course, still another reason for reading about the conquest of Canaan. It is a major event in Israel's history, and we can't ignore it any more than a student of American history can pass over such an unsavory episode as the Civil War. Also, there are some fine things along with all the gore: for example, God's admonition to Joshua in the first chapter: "Be strong and of good courage; be not frightened, neither be dismayed; for the Lord your God is with you wherever you go."

The second chapter contains one of those priceless vignettes which abound in the Bible. It is the story of two Israelite spies who were almost caught by the enemy, but escaped after finding refuge in a prostitute's home.

In chapter 3, the Israelites cross the Jordan to begin the invasion of Canaan. The account says that the waters of the river were miraculously parted to enable them to pass. This may be history, but many scholars suspect it is a late addition to the story, reflecting the growth of a legend which sought to turn Joshua into a "second Moses." What Moses did at the Sea of Reeds, Joshua must do at the Jordan.*

What happened after the crossing of the Jordan has been immortalized in a great Negro spiritual, "Joshua Fit the Battle of Jericho." This was no tank town that the Israelites assaulted. Jericho was the oldest city on earth. Modern archaeological explorations have confirmed that its origins as a city date back to about 9000 B.C. Following instructions given to him by an angel of the Lord, Joshua marched the Israelites around the city once a day for six days. Looking down at the motley band of nomads from the safety of their high and seemingly impregnable walls, the citizens of Jericho must have thought this a strange kind of siege indeed. On the seventh day, the Israelites marched around the city seven times, with priests blowing high-pitched trumpets made from

* There are other places in the Book of Joshua where the same kind of brushwork can be detected. In Joshua 5:13–15, an angel addresses Joshua in the very words that Moses heard from the burning bush. In Joshua 8:32, we read of Joshua carving the Law (i.e., the Ten Commandments) on tablets of stone.

hollowed-out rams' horns. "And at the seventh time, when the priests had blown the trumpets, Joshua said to the people, 'Shout, for the Lord has given you the city.' . . . So the people shouted, and the trumpets were blown . . . and the wall fell down flat, so that the people went up into the city, every man straight before him, and they took the city" (Joshua 6:16, 20).

Chapter 7 is another vignette about a man named Achan who yielded to the temptation to do a little private looting. The moral of the story is really the theme of the whole book of Joshua: when the Israelites obey God, they prosper; when they disobey, they get into trouble. This story also underscores a fact that helps to mitigate our horror at the Israelite policy of killing all men, women, and children, destroying all livestock, and razing all buildings in the cities which they captured. In pursuing this ruthless scorched earth policy, the Israelites were doing what they thought God wanted them to do—making sure that their Promised Land would not be contaminated by any remnants of a culture that had worshiped other gods. There was no element of private greed or revenge in their motivation. They destroyed with the dispassionate efficiency of men who are convinced they are waging a holy crusade.

I urge that you persevere through chapter 10, where you will come to the report of God's stoning the Amorites from heaven. After that, you can skip chapters 11 through 22, but I do commend to your attention the final chapters, 23 and 24, in which Joshua gives his farewell address to the Israelites, and confronts them with the famous challenge:

"Choose this day whom you will serve . . . but as for me and my house, we will serve the Lord."

THE JUDGES

The Israelite invasion of Canaan took place about 1250 B.C. The Book of Joshua gives the impression that it took only one generation to complete the conquest of the previous inhabitants and leave Israel in undisputed control of the Promised Land. Actually, it took much longer. In fact, it was not until the time of the great King David, 250 years later, that the Israelites achieved a firm and uncontested grip on the land. For generations after Joshua's death, the various tribes of Israel were involved in intermittent conflict with Canaanite cities that had successfully resisted subjugation, as well as with neighboring peoples such as the Moabites, Ammonites, Midianites, and Philistines. The latter, in particular, gave the Israelites a bad time. The Philistines were a non-Semitic people who had emigrated from Crete to establish five thriving cities along the coastal plain of Palestine south of Joppa. They were great warriors and had superior weapons—including horse-drawn chariots and suits of armor—which gave them an advantage over the Israelites in battle. For long periods of time, the Philistines were the real rulers of Canaan, exacting tribute from the Israelites.

The seventh book of the Old Testament, JUDGES, is a colorful collection of folk stories about some of the Israelite heroes who emerged during the centuries of strife and turmoil that elapsed between the invasion of Canaan and the final emergence of a powerful Hebrew empire under David.

During this period, Israel had no national leader such as Moses or Joshua. Every tribe fended for itself, and government, such as it was, was in the hands of men called *shophetim,* or judges. John J. Dougherty, a noted

Catholic Biblical scholar, points out that these men "were not judges in the sense of magistrates, but in the sense of military leaders. They were leaders of the tribes in time of trouble." Their exploits, recorded in the Book of Judges, make fascinating reading, particularly if you bear in mind Dougherty's warning that "not all the stories need be taken as literal history. Some of them obviously belong to the genre of sagas or legends."

The unknown editor of Judges was not interested solely in collecting folklore. He had a moral lesson which he wanted to impart. It is implicit in each of the stories, and is stated explicitly in the second chapter of his book.

> The people of Israel did what was evil in the sight of the Lord. . . . They forsook the God of their fathers who had brought them out of Egypt, and they went after other gods, from among the gods of the peoples who were around them.

Their lapse into the idolatry of the pagan culture which surrounded them was swiftly punished.

> The anger of the Lord was kindled against Israel, and he gave them over to plunderers, who plundered them; and he sold them into the power of their enemies round about, so that they could no longer withstand their enemies. Whenever they marched out, the hand of the Lord was against them as the Lord had warned . . . and they were in sore straits.

But God did not finally despair of his people. Despite their wicked ways, he still loved them, and heeded their plight. So from time to time,

> The Lord raised up judges, who saved the people out of the power of those who plundered them. . . .

Whenever the Lord raised up judges for them, the Lord was with the judge, and he saved them from the hand of their enemies all the days of the judge; for the Lord was moved to pity by their groaning because of those who afflicted and oppressed them.

But the Israelites were fickle.

As soon as a good judge died, "they turned back and behaved worse than their fathers, going after other gods . . . they did not drop any of their practices or their stubborn ways."

I have quoted this passage (Judges 2:11–19) at length because it represents such a tremendous advance in spiritual insight over the tribal-god morality of the Book of Joshua. The author of Judges is no narrow-minded chauvinist. He sees the sins as well as the glories of his nation, and he is asking, in effect, "How can we be so foolish as to disobey and forget God, after all He's done for us?" It is still a good question.

But the author of Judges is much too good a storyteller to labor his moral as hard as I'm laboring it for him here. This is one of the most readable and thoroughly delightful books of the Bible.

I suggest you start at chapter 4. It supposedly tells about a judge named Barak, but he is completely overshadowed in the story by two strong-minded women. One is a prophetess named Deborah, who goads Barak into action. The other is a courageous housewife named Jael who does in the commander of the enemy army in a crude but highly effective manner.

In chapter 5, you'll find Deborah's victory song, which is one of the oldest and finest pieces of Hebrew poetry in existence.

Chapters 6, 7, and 8 recount the exploits of Gideon, "a mighty man of valor" whom God raised up to free the Israelites from the oppressive yoke of the Midianites. I don't want to spoil any of these stories for you by giving away their plots, so I won't tell you the stratagems by which Gideon routed the foe. But I think you'll agree, after reading them, that even if you make allowances for a certain amount of legendary heightening, Gideon was one of the most imaginative generals in history.

The most heartbreaking story in the Bible is told in chapter 11. It is the story of Jephthah and his daughter. Its tragic ending is a stark reminder that Israel was still at a fairly primitive stage of religious development, in which human sacrifice was sometimes practiced, and vows were held to be sacred and unbreakable. It will help you to appreciate the poignancy of the story if you know that to die childless was considered the ultimate disaster that could befall an Israelite woman.

SAMSON

After such a depressing tale, it is a relief to come to the story of Samson, the Paul Bunyan of ancient Israel. His robust achievements in bed and battle are celebrated in chapters 13, 14, 15, and 16. Samson was a man of incredible physical strength, but he was very weak in the head, especially where women were concerned. There is an unforgettable vignette in chapter 16 which illuminates his character and underscores his principal enthusiasms:

> Samson went to Gaza, and there he saw a harlot, and went in to her. The Gazites were told, "Samson has come here," and they surrounded the place and lay in wait for him all night at the gate of the city.

They kept quiet all night, saying, "Let us wait till the light of the morning; then we will kill him." But Samson lay till midnight, and at midnight, he arose and took hold of the doors of the gate of the city and the two posts, and pulled them up, bar and all, and put them on his shoulders, and carried them to the top of the hill that is before Hebron.

You already know, of course, that Samson is finally gulled by a Philistine Mata Hari named Delilah. The Bible's version of how she played him for a sucker is much more believable than Cecil B. De Mille's. In it we encounter for the first time in any of the world's literature a line that has done yeoman service in novels, poems, plays, and soap operas ever since:

"And she said to him, 'How can you say, "I love you," when your heart is not with me?'"

Every husband will find himself sympathizing with the poor guy in the next verse:

"And when she pressed him hard with her words day after day, and urged him, his soul was vexed to death."

There are five more chapters (17 to 21) to the Book of Judges, but you can pass them over if you wish. They're rather anticlimactic.

ISRAEL BECOMES A KINGDOM

Late in the period of the Judges, about 1050 B.C., Israel again found a ruler who was strong enough to unite the whole nation. His name was Samuel. Like Moses, he was at once a prophet and a political leader. His story is told in the ninth book of the Old Testament, which is called 1 SAMUEL. (There also is a 2 SAMUEL, which is all about David rather than Samuel. The two books bearing the name of Samuel were originally one manuscript in Hebrew. They were divided into their present format during the sixteenth century, for no particularly good reason.)

If you've ever attended Sunday School, the chances are you've heard about Samuel's birth and boyhood. The story begins in chapter 1 of 1 Samuel with his mother Hannah praying for a son to remove the stigma of her barrenness, and promising to dedicate him to God's service. Hannah's song of thanksgiving after her prayer is answered (recorded in chapter 2) is of special interest as a literary model for the famed Magnificat of the Virgin Mary:

My heart exults in the Lord;
my strength is exalted in the Lord.
My mouth derides my enemies,
    because I rejoice in thy salvation.

There is none holy like the Lord,
    there is none besides thee;
    there is no rock like our God.
Talk no more so very proudly,
    let not arrogance come from your mouth;
    for the Lord is a God of knowledge,
    and by him actions are weighed.
The bows of the mighty are broken,
    but the feeble gird on strength.
Those who were full have hired themselves out for bread,
    but those who were hungry have ceased to hunger.
The barren has borne seven
    but she who has many children is forlorn.
The Lord kills and brings to life;
    he brings down to Sheol and raises up.

The Lord makes poor and makes rich;
   he brings low, he also exalts.
He raises up the poor from the dust;
   he lifts the needy from the ash heap,
to make them sit with princes
   and inherit a seat of honor.
For the pillars of the earth are the Lord's,
   and on them he has set the world.

He will guard the feet of his faithful ones;
   but the wicked shall be cut off in darkness;
   for not by might shall a man prevail.
The adversaries of the Lord shall be broken to pieces;
   against them he will thunder in heaven.
The Lord will judge the ends of the earth;
   he will give strength to his king,
   and exalt the power of his anointed.

(1 Samuel 2:1–10)

Chapter 3 opens with one of those priceless Biblical sentences which make every author envious because they manage to say so much so well in so few words:

"And the word of the Lord was rare in those days: there was no frequent vision."

SAMUEL

Samuel is still a young boy. In keeping with his mother's promise, he has been dedicated to God's service, and is living at the temple with the old high priest, Eli. One night, after retiring, Samuel hears his name called, and he thinks the aging priest has summoned him. But Eli says, "I did not call, my son; lie down again." Three times the scene is repeated, until Eli finally gets the point. He tells Samuel that if he hears the voice again, he should reply:

"Speak, Lord, for thy servant hears." The call is repeated, and this time Samuel responds as Eli has told him. The Lord's message is grim: Eli's house is doomed, because of the wickedness of Eli's sons (whose transgressions include seducing women who come to the temple to worship). Samuel faithfully relays the message to Eli. And old Eli wins an imperishable place in the Biblical record by uttering a single sentence of magnificent submission:

"It is the Lord; let him do what seems good to him."

We are told at the end of chapter 3 that "Samuel grew, and the Lord was with him and let none of his words fall to the ground." After he attained manhood, he became *de facto* head of the nation. According to 1 Samuel 7:15 he "judged Israel all the days of his life." You need not read all the details of his career as a judge. For Samuel is important in Israel's history primarily as a transitional figure. It was he who anointed Israel's first king. You can follow the essential thread of the story quite well by skipping from chapter 3 to chapter 8, in which we are introduced to one of the most tragic personalities of the Bible, King Saul.

SAUL

The remainder of 1 Samuel is the story of Saul's reign as Israel's first king. I think you will want to read it right through. It is an absorbing narrative about a striking young man ("There was not a man among the people of Israel more handsome than he; from his shoulders upward he was taller than any of the people") who was thrust into heavy responsibilities which he did not seek. He is valorous in battle and wins the adulation of the people. But Israel is, as always, fickle. A younger military hero named David comes along, and soon the street crowds are shouting,

> Saul has slain his thousands,
> and David his ten thousands.

Saul's jealousy of David, vividly described in the last fourteen chapters of 1 Samuel, drives him at last into the intensely suspicious type of madness which modern psychiatry knows as paranoia. He tries to kill David, but David escapes into the wilderness, and Saul is unable to capture him, even though he scours the countryside with his army. Saul's jealous torment is heightened by the knowledge that David has won over his own children. Saul's son, Jonathan, is David's best friend, and Saul's daughter, Michal, is David's adoring young bride.

The tragedy of Saul mounts to a climax when Samuel turns against the king he anointed, condemning Saul for his failure to butcher all of the Amalekites whom he had defeated in battle.* Saul confesses that he disobeyed the prophet's orders not out of compassion for the captives, but "because I feared the people and obeyed their voice." Saul begs forgiveness but Samuel tells him sternly that "you have rejected the word of the Lord, and the Lord has rejected you. . . ."

In chapter 28, we find the wretched king creeping out of his palace at night in disguise to consult a medium, the witch of Endor. This episode, which is clearly to be read as legend rather than history, vividly portrays Saul's sense of abandonment. "I am in great distress," he says. "God

---

* The notion that God would be furious with Saul for sparing lives is hard for us to swallow, but remember what was said in the earlier discussion of Joshua (pages 146 ff.). Israel's ideas about God's attitude toward prisoners of war remained very primitive right through the reign of David.

has turned away from me and answers me no more, either by prophets or by dreams." But Samuel, even when summoned back from the grave, remains unmoved and unforgiving. He pronounces Saul's doom, and Saul collapses on the ground. The tenderness with which the medium ministers to him shows that she was a far cry from our modern image of a witch.

Skip chapters 29 and 30 for now. They are part of David's story, which we're coming to later. To get the full impact of Saul's final debacle, you must go directly from the scene at the home of the witch of Endor to chapter 31, in which Saul sees his army defeated, his sons slain, and his kingdom overrun. He can't even persuade one of his men to run him through with a sword so that he may die a soldier's death. He has to do it himself.

I have traced Saul's story at this length because I think that the author of 1 Samuel was biased against Saul and does not treat him quite fairly. The facts are all there, but they have been subjected to such a heavily pro-David slant that you need to do some reading between the lines to see that Saul was not an evil man but one stalked by tragedy.

DAVID

The story of David begins in 1 Samuel 16, continues throughout 2 Samuel, and concludes in 1 Kings 2. It is one of the finest biographies ever written, and could only have come from the pen of an eyewitness. Some scholars are inclined to think that the author may have been a priest named Abiathar, who figures in the story in a minor but persistent way. But this is only a guess, and there is no way we can ever be sure who is responsible for this magnificent warts-and-all portrait of one of the most complex

The Empire of David

and attractive human beings who ever walked across the stage of history.

We first encounter David in 1 Samuel 16 as a shepherd boy whom God has pointed out to Samuel as Saul's destined successor on the throne of Israel. Later in the same chapter, we are told that David was brought to Saul's court to function as a sort of bard, providing soft background music when the king was in a black mood. This is plausible, because we know from other accounts that David was an expert musician. (His instrument was *not* the harp, as Sunday School stories used to say, but a lyre, a U-shaped affair with six strings.) However, this account of David's career as a musician in Saul's court does not square with 1 Samuel 16:48–57, which indicates that Saul met David for the first time after the Goliath episode. What we obviously have here is another of the many cases in which Biblical editors have faithfully preserved two conflicting traditions without trying to choose between them.

It makes a more satisfying narrative if we begin the story of David with 1 Samuel 17, which describes the slaying of the Philistine giant Goliath. This is a great anecdote, and its impact on the imagination is attested by the vast amount of art it has inspired, including Michelangelo's immortal statue of the shepherd boy with his sling. There is no reason to doubt the essential historicity of the story although some of the details have been subjected to legendary exaggeration. Goliath's dimensions as given in the Bible would translate to a height of about ten feet and the weight of his armor to more than 300 pounds.

David was blessed with a charismatic personality. Everyone liked him. Men admired him and readily accepted him as their leader. (Even Saul liked him at first—see 1 Samuel 16:21.) Women found him irresistibly attractive. David's ability to make and keep friends is reflected in his relationship with Saul's son, Jonathan, who loved David "as his own soul" and remained loyal to him even when the king was trying to track him down and kill him (see 1 Samuel 20, for example).

David was a born leader. Even when he was hiding out in the wilderness, a fugitive from the king's wrath, he attracted a large and loyal following. "Everyone who was in distress, and everyone who was in debt, and everyone who was discontented, gathered to him; and he became captain over them," says 1 Samuel 22:2. Finally, he had a band of some 400 outcasts and outlaws. Anticipating Robin Hood by 3000 years, they plundered the rich and protected the poor, and kept on the move to avoid King Saul's search parties.

David was magnanimous. Twice he caught Saul completely off guard (on one occasion, the ever-realistic Bible notes, Saul was in a cave "relieving himself") and could have killed him easily. But on each occasion, David spared the life of the man who was trying so hard to kill him.

But David also could get tough. The twenty-fifth chapter of 1 Samuel contains a delightful vignette about a stingy shepherd named Nabal who accepted the protection of David's band, but refused to come through with food when David sent out a foraging party to replenish the larder. David set out immediately at the head of a raiding party to destroy Nabal and seize his belongings. But Nabal's wife, Abigail, was a smart woman. She heard of her husband's surly reply to David's envoys, and guessing what would come next, she hastily loaded a convoy of donkeys with "two hundred loaves, and two skins of wine, and five sheep ready dressed, and five measures of parched grain, and a hundred clusters of raisins, and two hundred cakes of figs," and set out to intercept the raiding party. David accepted the friendship offering and—characteristically—was enchanted by the lady herself. When he heard a few days later that her husband had been carried off by an untimely death, David sent for her "to make her his wife." And Abigail, like every other woman whom David ever summoned, "made haste" to his arms.

David was a good politician. After Saul's death, he set his sights on the throne, but he had to go slow. First, he became ruler over Judah, the southern half of the country. Saul's son, Ish-bosheth, had been proclaimed king in the Northern Kingdom, which is referred to in the Bible as Israel. Conflict was inevitable, and it came. "There was a long war between the house of Saul and the house of David; and David grew stronger and stronger, while the house of Saul became weaker and weaker." Finally, Ish-bosheth's general, Abner, defected to David, and Ish-bosheth was murdered in his bed by traitors who hoped to curry favor with David. But David was shrewd enough to know that he would never sit securely on a throne which he attained by such measures. So instead of rewarding the assassins who brought him Ish-bosheth's head, David had them executed for their crime. That made a big hit with the Important People in Israel, and in no time at all a delegation was calling on David and pleading with him to accept the kingship of Israel. He graciously obliged them.

David's first move, after both parts of the country were united under his rule, was to find himself a neutral capital city, much as the founding fathers of the United States established a new Federal City on the Potomac River that was identified neither with the northern nor with the southern states. His choice was the ancient city of Jerusalem, which had resisted Israelite conquest since the invasion of Canaan. David's general, Joab, led an attack party into Jerusalem by following an underground water tunnel. The city capitulated, and became David's private domain. He set up his capital there, built himself an impressive palace (with help from a friendly Phoenician king who had lots of lumber to export), and tried to rename it "the City of David" or, as we would say today, Davidsburg.

David was a first-rate military leader. His armies subdued the Philistines, making them vassals of the Israelites. He also conquered neighboring tribes such as the Moabites and extended his rule from the Euphrates River in the north to the boundaries of Egypt in the south. By the end of his forty-year reign, he was absolute master of the most powerful empire in the Middle Eastern world of his day. (It should be noted, however, that this pre-eminent position was attainable only because Egypt and Assyria were in a state of demoralization.) Tribute flowed into Jerusalem from all over the "Fertile Crescent" of the Middle East, and the whole country waxed rich and prosperous.

It is very rare to find a great warrior who is also a great poet. But David was both. He definitely did *not* write all the Psalms which the King James Version attributes to him. But he probably did write some. And even if he had no other credentials as a poet, his fame would rest secure on one work of art that was indubitably his—the lament for Saul and Jonathan recorded in 2 Samuel 1:

Thy glory, O Israel, is slain upon thy high places!
How are the mighty fallen!
Tell it not in Gath, publish it not in the streets of
    Ashkelon;

lest the daughters of the Philistines rejoice,
lest the daughters of the uncircumcised exult.
Ye mountains of Gilboa, let there be no dew or rain upon
you,
nor upsurging of the deep!
For there the shield of the mighty was defiled,
the shield of Saul, not anointed with oil.
From the blood of the slain,
from the fat of the mighty,
the bow of Jonathan turned not back,
and the sword of Saul returned not empty.
Saul and Jonathan, beloved and lovely!
In life and in death they were not divided;
they were swifter than eagles,
they were stronger than lions.
Ye daughters of Israel, weep over Saul,
who clothed you daintily in scarlet,
who put ornaments of gold upon your apparel.
How are the mighty fallen
in the midst of the battle!
Jonathan lies slain upon thy high places.
I am distressed for you, my brother Jonathan;
very pleasant have you been to me;
your love to me was wonderful,
passing the love of women.
How are the mighty fallen,
and the weapons of war perished!

Poet, musician, warrior, king—was there *nothing* that
David couldn't do? Yes. He couldn't govern his appetite
for women. And he couldn't rule his own children.

"In the spring of the year, the time when kings go forth
to battle . . ." So begins the story of David and Bathsheba, which is recorded in the eleventh and twelfth

chapters of 2 Samuel. No paraphrase can possibly improve upon the Biblical account, so I will repress the temptation to retell it here. In this story, Israel's greatest king is embroiled in a series of despicable crimes, and it is to the credit of his biographer that no attempt is made to gloss over, alibi, or explain away his conduct. The only hero of this episode is the prophet Nathan, who boldly confronts the king and denounces his sin to his face.

But even in this moment of ultimate degradation, David displays a saving grace. "I have sinned against the Lord," he says. Think for a moment how difficult it was for the absolute monarch to confess publicly that he had done wrong. But David did confess, and repented publicly, and meekly accepted the punishment which God administered to him. Thus we see in the same story both extremes of David's character—his capacity for ruthless self-indulgence, and his genuine desire to serve the Lord.

David's greatest failure was as a parent. His indulgent attitude toward his offspring is memorably described in a single sentence of 2 Kings which says of his son, Adonijah: "His father had never at any time displeased him by asking, 'Why have you done thus and so?'"

David reaped the inevitable consequence of this method of child-rearing when his son Absalom rose in revolt against him, and tried to seize his throne. The story of Absalom's revolution is told in 2 Samuel 13 through 20. It will be of interest to modern parents to know that Absalom wore his hair very long. According to 2 Samuel 14:26, he got a haircut only once a year. Whether all that hair made him ornery, or whether he was just a spoiled brat looking for trouble, we do not know. But he gave his father a very bad time, and came close to unseating him. It was the hair that finally did Absalom in. He was riding through a forest, during the climactic battle, when his hair got entangled in the branches of a tree. He hung there helpless until David's general Joab came along and drove darts into his heart.

Joab's action was in strict violation of David's orders. Even after his son had risen in revolt and was about to take his kingdom, David instructed his men to "deal gently for my sake with the young man Absalom." And when the news of Absalom's death reached David, "the king was deeply moved, and went up to the chamber over the gate, and wept; and as he went he said, 'O my son Absalom, my son, my son Absalom! Would I had died instead of you, O Absalom, my son, my son.'"

David ruled over Israel from 1000 to 960 B.C. His last days are poignantly described in the first chapter of 1 Kings. David had reached the age of seventy-three, which was very old for his time. I cannot help but prefer the language of the King James Version here:

"Now King David was old and stricken in years; and they covered him with clothes, but he gat no heat."

His courtiers, remembering his lifelong enthusiasm for female company, brought him a young girl to share his bed.

> So they sought for a fair damsel throughout all the coasts of Israel, and found Abishag, a Shunammite, and brought her to the king.
>
> And the damsel was very fair, and cherished the king, and ministered to him.
>
> But the king knew her not.

I predict you will like David. Whatever his faults and foibles, he was a warm-hearted man who had the essential attributes of greatness. His deepest motivation, which survived all the temptations of power and which ultimately triumphed over all of his baser instincts, was a genuine love of God. His faith did not consist in giving lip-service to pious doctrines. It was the kind of faith that issued in obedient actions—from going forth to fight a giant to governing a kingdom. His unshakable trust in God is beautifully expressed in the hymn of praise recorded in the twenty-second chapter of 2 Samuel:

The Lord is my rock, and my fortress, and my deliverer,
My God, my rock, in whom I take refuge,
My shield and the horn of my salvation,
My stronghold and my refuge . . .
I call upon the Lord, who is worthy to be praised,
And I am saved from my enemies.

SOLOMON

David's sons did not wait until he was gone to squabble over the succession. The struggle for the throne broke out while the aged king was still lingering on his deathbed. The story is told in the FIRST BOOK OF KINGS.

"Now Adonijah the son of Haggith exalted himself, saying, 'I will be king.'" Adonijah, as the eldest son, had a good claim to the crown. He also had powerful supporters, including Joab, the head of the armed forces, and Abiathar, the chief priest. But this formidable coalition was defeated by a woman—the beautiful Bathsheba, David's favorite wife.

Bathsheba's first-born son—the issue of her adultery with David—had died soon after birth. She bore David one more son. His name was Solomon, and Bathsheba was determined that he inherit the kingdom. During a romantic moment, she extracted from her ardent husband a promise that Solomon would be his heir. When Adonijah made a grab for the throne, Bathsheba went to the bedchamber of the senile David and reminded him of his promise:

> My lord, you swore to your maidservant by the Lord your God saying, 'Solomon your son shall reign after me, and he shall sit upon my throne.' And now, behold, Adonijah is king, although you, my lord the king, do not know it."

David's reaction was exactly what Bathsheba anticipated. Bestirring his aged bones for one last burst of action, he called in the functionaries of the court and issued a royal decree: Solomon was to be publicly anointed at once. "And he shall come and sit upon my throne; for he shall be king in my stead; and I have appointed him to be ruler over Israel and over Judah."

Thus Solomon comes on the stage of history in the unflattering role of Mama's boy. One cannot help wondering whether this was in David's mind when he summoned Solomon to his deathbed and admonished him: "Be strong, and show yourself a man."

Solomon followed the paternal advice. Within a short time after David's death, Solomon had firmly established his grip on the kingdom by executing Adonijah and Joab, and sending Abiathar into exile.

You will find a colorful account of Solomon's career in the first eleven chapters of 1 Kings. Solomon's forty-year reign was the golden age of the Hebrews' United Kingdom. "Judah and Israel were as many as the sand by the sea; they ate and drank and were happy . . . every man under his vine and under his fig tree, all the days of Solomon."

David's military conquests had created an extensive empire. "Solomon ruled over all the kingdoms from the

Euphrates to the land of the Philistines and to the border of Egypt." Solomon never had to fight a war, partly because the neighboring empires of Egypt and Assyria were going through periods of internal weakness, and partly because he built up a powerful defense force, which discouraged attacks on his territory. David had won the empire with an army of foot soldiers. But Solomon, anticipating modern military doctrine, concentrated on building up a highly mobile armored force. He eventually was able to field 12,000 horsemen and 1400 chariots—a formidable array for his time. Solomon's decision to concentrate on cavalry was good strategy in a country with long, exposed borders. But it was not dictated entirely by military considerations. Solomon loved horses. According to 1 Kings 10:28 he imported swift steeds from as far away as Egypt and Asia Minor, and paid high prices for them.

Solomon's empire straddled the world's busiest trade route, and Solomon took full advantage of the era of peace to establish a far-flung commerce. He sent caravans overland to Egypt, Arabia and Mesopotamia, and built a fleet of ships which ranged into distant parts of the Mediterranean. The exotic cargoes which flowed into the kingdom are described in a sentence that has been envied by generations of poets:

"Once every three years the ships of Tarshish used to come,
"Bringing gold, silver, ivory, apes, and peacocks."

Solomon became fabulously rich. According to 1 Kings 10:14 his annual income, in gold alone, came to 666 talents. A talent of gold was worth about $30,000; 666 talents figures out to about $20 million, which was an almost incredible fortune at the price levels prevailing in that period. The opulence of Solomon's court is summed up in two brief sentences: "All of King Solomon's drinking vessels were of gold. None were of silver, it was not considered as anything in the days of Solomon."

Like many other rich men, before and since, Solomon was bitten by the building bug. His first big project was the erection of a temple in Jerusalem. The details of the construction are given, in a tone of awe, in chapters 5 and 6 of 1 Kings. The dimensions of the temple, which are given in the ancient Hebrew unit of linear measurement, the cubit, were approximately ninety feet in length, thirty feet in width, and forty-five feet in height.

No contemporary congregation has ever embarked on a church-building program with a greater contempt for cost than Solomon displayed in the lavish design and furnishing of the temple. He imported expensive lumber—cedar and cypress from the forests of Lebanon—for which he paid a Phoenician king 125,000 bushels of wheat and one million gallons of olive oil. He imposed heavy taxes and drafted 180,000 men into forced-labor battalions.

It took seven years to complete the temple. When the last bit of gold inlay was in place, the Israelites breathed a sigh of relief. But it was entirely premature.

Solomon now set about building a house for himself which was larger and grander in every way than the one he had built for Jehovah. "Solomon was building his own house thirteen years," says the author of 1 Kings. The palace was nearly twice the size of the temple—150 feet long, 75 feet wide, 45 feet high. Even if one allows for a certain amount of exaggeration in the description of the palace and its contents (in 1 Kings 7), it must have been one of the most ornate and extravagant buildings ever put up. There can't have been many homes in which gold was used for wallpaper.

The Biblical descriptions of Solomon's opulence remind us that it is tempting in every age to measure a man's success in terms of the material possessions he has managed to pile up. When we find ourselves disapproving of this extravagant, self-indulgent king, we may pause to remember that we also live in the most pampered society the world has ever known, and that a middle-class American family enjoys luxuries that only kings could afford in Solomon's day.

Solomon's determination to outshine all of the other Oriental potentates of his day also found expression in the size of his harem. He had a particular taste, we are told in 1 Kings 11, for "foreign women." Some of his foreign wives—for example, the daughter of the Pharaoh of Egypt —obviously were acquired for diplomatic reasons, that is, to cement alliances with the powerful neighbors. But Solomon also stocked his harem with "Moabite, Ammonite, Edomite, Sidonian, and Hittite women." And he never seemed to know when enough was enough. He ultimately accumulated 700 wives and 300 concubines.

But Solomon was destined to be remembered best neither for his wealth nor for his wives, but for his wisdom. And, we are told in the third chapter of 1 Kings, this was his deliberate choice.

The biographer relates that God appeared to Solomon in a dream and offered to give him anything he asked. Instead of asking for wealth or power or long life, Solomon asked for wisdom. God was so impressed that he gave Solomon not only "a wise and discerning mind" but also "riches and honor so that no other king shall compare with you."

Although this story probably belongs to the same class of literature as the one about George Washington and the

cherry tree, it is nonetheless very significant. The impact
of an historical figure on his own time is often best reflected in the legends that grow up about him. Hebrew
legend came to depict Solomon as the "wisest" man who
ever lived. This characterization will be misleading if
you think of wisdom in its contemporary connotation of
profound insight into the human condition. In Hebrew
usage, a wise man was one who had a keen intelligence
and a large store of knowledge. In many respects, as we
will see shortly, Solomon was not truly wise in the sense
of being sagacious. In fact, he did some very stupid
things, which ultimately led to the downfall of his empire.
But he was unquestionably the Thomas Jefferson of his
time—a many-sided intellectual whose genius awed ordinary men.

Like Jefferson, he was interested in architecture, music,
literature, and science as well as the art of government.
He was a careful student of nature: 1 Kings 4:33 says
that he was knowledgeable about all kinds of trees, plants,
animals, birds, reptiles and fish. He was credited with
composing 1005 songs, which sounds rather like an exaggeration, but which is the kind of claim that would not be
made had he not been well-known as a composer. He
also was said to have uttered 3000 epigrams, or proverbs.
Some of his sayings may be included in the Old Testament
book of Proverbs.*

Solomon's reputation as a wise man was also based in
part on his penetrating judicial decisions. One of his famous judgments is recorded in 1 Kings 3:16–27.

* The entire book of Proverbs is traditionally ascribed to Solomon's authorship, as are three other Biblical books: the Song of Solomon, Ec-
clesiastes, and the Wisdom of Solomon. But most scholars regard these
ascriptions as simply a literary convention—"wisdom" books being attributed to the man who is the symbol of Hebrew wisdom. We'll go into
all this in more detail when we come to these books later.

Then two harlots came to the king and stood before him.

The one woman said, "Oh, my lord, this woman and I dwell in the same house; and I gave birth to a child while she was in the house. Then on the third day after I was delivered, this woman also gave birth; and we were alone; there was no one else with us in the house, only we two were in the house.

And this woman's son died in the night, because she lay on it. And she arose at midnight, and took my son from beside me, while your maidservant slept, and laid it in her bosom, and laid her dead son in my bosom.

When I rose in the morning to nurse my child, behold, it was dead; but when I looked at it closely in the morning, behold, it was not the child that I had borne."

But the other woman said, "No, the living child is mine, and the dead child is yours." The first said, "No, the dead child is yours, and the living child is mine." Thus they spoke before the king.

Then the king said, "The one says, 'This is my son that is alive, and your son is dead'; and the other says, 'No; but your son is dead, and my son is the living one.'"

And the king said, "Bring me a sword." So a sword was brought before the king.

And the king said, "Divide the living child in two, and give half to the one, and half to the other."

Then the woman whose son was alive said to the king, because her heart yearned for her son, "Oh, my lord, give her the living child, and by no means slay it." But the other said, "It shall be neither mine nor yours; divide it."

Then the king answered and said, "Give the living
child to the first woman, and by no means slay it;
she is its mother."

Solomon's fame spread far and wide. It aroused the
womanly curiosity of the Queen of Sheba, who ruled over
the wealthy little country in the southwestern part of the
Arabian peninsula which is known today as Yemen. She
decided to pay Solomon a visit, and test his wisdom with
"hard questions." "She came to Jerusalem with a very
great retinue, with camels bearing spices, and very much
gold and precious stones," says the author of 1 Kings.
This account of the visit in chapter 10 is one of the best-
known stories in the Bible, perhaps because he wisely
leaves many of the details to the reader's imagination.
And one can let his imagination run riot here without being likely to get far beyond the reality. The trek from
Sheba to Jerusalem was more than 1200 miles, so that
the Queen's camel caravan must have been on the road,
going and coming, for many months. Her "very great
retinue" probably required at least 1000 camels for trans-
portation. And beyond the queenly gifts which she
brought to Solomon, it was necessary to bring enough
food for the long journey, including herds of sheep.

One would like to know what "hard questions" the
Queen put to Solomon. Perhaps they were riddles—a favorite way of testing intelligence in the Middle East. But
we are told only that the Queen was greatly impressed,
not only by Solomon's wisdom, but also by the magnifi-
cence of his palace.

"I did not believe the reports until I came and my own
eyes had seen it," said the dark-eyed Arabian princess who
was no slouch at the ancient female art of flattery. "Be-

hold, the half was not told me; your wisdom and prosperity surpass the report which I had heard. Happy are your wives!"

If the latter remark is construed as a not-very-subtle hint, it can also be conjectured that Solomon was not slow to take her up on it. The Bible is silent on the point, but tradition holds that the Queen of Sheba had a son by Solomon, whom she named Menelek. He is proudly claimed as an ancestor by the present royal house of Ethiopia, which may be the reason why many people mistakenly think that the Queen of Sheba came from Ethiopia.

Solomon's appetite for "foreign women" led him at last into the one sin which his biographer—however sycophantic—could not condone. "When Solomon was old, his wives turned away his heart after other gods; and his heart was not wholly true to the Lord his God, as was the heart of David his father," says the author of 1 Kings. In an effort to keep peace in his vast harem, Solomon let his foreign wives continue to worship their old tribal gods. Inevitably, his court became a mélange of pagan rites. In time, even Solomon himself, who had begun his reign with such pious protestations of devotion to God, succumbed to the polytheism and idolatry which infested his sumptuous palace. Thus "Solomon did what was evil in the sight of the Lord" and introduced dry rot into the very heart of his outwardly affluent kingdom.

Compromising Israel's religion was not the only folly of which Solomon was guilty. His extravagances, and particularly the heavy taxes and forced labor required by his building program, stirred deep resentment in the people. The blowup did not come in his time. Like another vain and extravagant king, Louis XV of France, Solomon managed to keep the show going until he died. But he might well have said with Louis, *Après moi le déluge* [After me, the flood].

THE DECLINE AND FALL
OF THE HEBREW EMPIRE

Solomon died in 922 B.C., and was succeeded by his son Rehoboam. The kingdom was seething with discontent over the ruthless exactions of money, produce, and labor required to maintain Solomon in all his glory. But humble people are perennial optimists, and the exploited children of Israel hoped that things would be different with a new king on the throne. Rehoboam could have pulled the fat out of the fire, had he been smart enough to sense the mood of his people, and to respond to it.

But Rehoboam was a classic example of a type of king all too common in history. He was pig-headed.

The twelfth chapter of 1 Kings tells how "all the assembly of Israel" approached Rehoboam with a petition for the redress of grievances:

"Your father made our yoke heavy," they told the young king. "Now therefore lighten the hard service of your father and his heavy yoke upon us, and we will serve you."

Rehoboam's reply deserves to rank, in the annals of royal stupidity, alongside Marie Antoinette's reply when she was told that the poor people of Paris had no bread: "Let them eat cake!"

"My father made your yoke heavy," said Rehoboam, "but I will add to your yoke. My father chastised you with whips, but I will chastise you with scorpions."

This proclamation of policy had the result which any good politician could have predicted. The northern part of the kingdom, Israel, repudiated Rehoboam's rule and seceded from the union established under David. Rehoboam continued to reign over the southern part of the kingdom, called Judah.

For the next 200 years, Israel and Judah existed as separate countries. Sometimes they were at war with one another; at other times they were military allies. Each had a few good kings, who governed wisely and acknowledged the lordship of Jehovah. Both had many bad kings, who—in a phrase that is reiterated like a refrain in the Biblical history of the period—"did what was evil in the sight of the Lord" and led their people into idolatry.

It is perhaps not easy for us today to appreciate the anguish and disgust which Biblical writers felt when they saw God's covenanted people lapsing into pagan ways. We take for granted the monotheistic concept which we inherited from Israel, and do not realize how often it came very near to being snuffed out by the polytheistic culture which always surrounded and often engulfed the Hebrew people. In our proud broad-mindedness, we also are inclined to forget that idol worship was not just a harmless blind spot of primitive peoples. It often had ghastly consequences.

The seventeenth chapter of the SECOND BOOK OF KINGS contains a succinct description of what really happened when the Hebrews turned their backs on "the Lord their God who had brought them up out of the land of Egypt."

"And they forsook all the commandments of the Lord their God, and made for themselves molten images. . . . And they burned their sons and their daughters as offerings, and used divination and sorcery."

The two pagan religions which gained the strongest hold over the apostate Hebrews of this period were Baal worship and the cult of the female goddess Astarte, who is usually referred to in the Biblical manuscripts as Asherah. Both of these pagan religions were imported from neighboring Phoenicia.

Baal was a fertility god represented by a statue in a seated position. In his lap burned the sacred fire, where children were burned as human sacrifices. Astarte, or Asherah, was the goddess of fertility. She was usually depicted as a naked, large-breasted woman with a serpent twined about her thighs. Male worshipers who entered a temple of Astarte found priestesses ready to serve as prostitutes. Women worshipers—including wives, mothers, and virgin daughters—were expected to give themselves to strangers as a token of their devotion to the goddess.

After many ups and downs, which are chronicled in great detail in the first and second books of Kings, the kingdom of Israel reached the end of the line in 722 B.C. The Assyrian Empire, expanding in all directions under the rule of the vigorous king Tiglath-pileser III, and his successors, conquered Israel, and carried its people into captivity. It was Assyrian policy to disperse a conquered people, scattering them far and wide in other countries so that there would be no danger of their reuniting and starting a revolt. This policy was carried out in Israel with such harsh efficiency that the northern tribes of the Hebrew people totally disappeared from history. They are sometimes referred to in literature as "the ten lost tribes of Israel" and have been the subject of much fascinating speculation over the centuries. It is a belief of the Mormon Church for example, that American Indians are descended from one of the Lost Tribes which somehow made it across to North America.

The kingdom of Judah managed to remain independent for another century and a half. Judah held off the Assyrians, usually by paying tribute, but occasionally by armed resistance, until the Assyrian Empire began to crumble from its own internal stresses at the end of the seventh century B.C. But the collapse of Assyria coincided with the rise of another expansionist empire, the Babylonian or Chaldean Empire. Under the able but ruthless King Nebuchadnezzar, Chaldean armies subjugated Judah in 587 B.C. The walls of Jerusalem, so long inviolate, were razed to the ground. Solomon's temple was sacked and burned, and most of the people were led away to Babylon as captives.

This tragic period of Hebrew history is chronicled in the latter half of 1 Kings and the entire book of 2 Kings. Unless you're an avid student of history, I see no great need in your wading through this generally dreary and often repetitious mass of material.

However, there is one great story embedded in it that you must not miss. It is the story of The Prophet and the Wicked Woman. You will find it in chapters 17, 18, 19, and 21 of 1 Kings. (Skip the twentieth chapter, which is a digression.)

The prophet's name was Elijah the Tishbite. He was a strong-minded man who had a habit of showing up in the royal court, clad in an animal-skin tunic and leather girdle, to denounce the king and queen for their misdeeds. The wicked woman was Queen Jezebel, a Phoenician princess who dominated her weak-willed husband, King Ahab of Israel, and just about everyone else except Elijah.

Both Elijah and Jezebel are fascinating characters, and you'll find no better narrative in the Bible than the story of their head-on clash of wills. At stake was the whole religious orientation of Israel. Jezebel was a devoted follower of Baal and Astarte, and was determined to convert

Israel to the worship of her Phoenician gods. To further
her proselytizing campaign, she imported 850 prophets
and priests from Tyre, the coastal city ruled by her father.
She made her husband build a temple for Baal and a
shrine dedicated to Astarte. Ahab didn't like to do this,
because he knew very well how Jehovah felt about foreign
gods, but he was no match for Jezebel's iron will and
would do anything to please her, or at least keep her quiet.

But Elijah was not so easily intimidated. He stalked
into the palace and bluntly notified Ahab that God would
send a drought upon Israel as punishment for apostasy.
His warning was borne out. The rains came no more, and
the parched land was brought to the edge of famine. At
this point, Elijah issued a challenge to Jezebel's big corps
of pagan prophets. Let us gather all the people of Israel
together at Mount Carmel, said Elijah, and see whose
deity is capable of breaking the drought. The Baalites
foolishly accepted the challenge.

When you read the story, in the eighteenth chapter of
1 Kings, let your mind's eye supply the background: the
huge crowd assembled at Mount Carmel, a high promon-
tory jutting out into the blue waters of the Mediterranean;
the long-haired, white-bearded prophet standing alone at
one simple altar; the horde of Baalite priests gathered
around the other. Hear the mocking tone of Elijah's voice
as he taunts the prophets of Baal by suggesting that they
should cry louder: he is asleep and must be awakened.
Note the fine touch of almost-arrogant confidence when
Elijah thrice drenches his altar wood with water before
calling down fire from heaven to consume it. The drama
builds up truly magnificent suspense in the final scene, as
Elijah waits for God to send the rainstorm that will vindi-
cate his faith. Seven times, he sends his servant to look out

to sea for any sign of a raincloud. Six times, the servant sees only bright blue sky. But on the seventh examination of the horizon, he sees "a little cloud, no bigger than a man's hand, rising out of the sea." And Elijah sends word to Ahab and Jezebel that they'd better hurry back to the palace or they'll get very wet.

If you've ever wondered how the name Jezebel became synonymous with vicious femininity, you'll find the answer in 1 Kings 21, which tells how the queen robbed a poor farmer named Naboth of his vineyard. Once again, the irate Elijah appears in court. And this time, he is concerned not with religious orthodoxy, but with social justice. He tells the king and queen to their face that they have sinned against a poor man, and therefore against God, and pronounces a horrible doom upon them. You will find the denouement of this story—in which Elijah's prophecy about the fate of Ahab and Jezebel is fulfilled —in 2 Kings 9:14–36. Incidentally, this passage also may make clear where our Puritan forebears got the notion that a "painted woman" was automatically wanton. Jezebel, like all Phoenician noblewomen of her time, used cosmetics. It was really an act of gallantry, which does her credit, that she put on make-up to confront her executioner.

The end of Elijah's story is found in the second chapter of 2 Kings, which preserves an ancient legend that he was spared from death and was taken to heaven aboard a fiery chariot. Aside from the fact that it inspired the great spiritual "Swing Low, Sweet Chariot," this story is significant primarily as an index of the very high place which Elijah held in the memory of his people. You will no doubt remember another story, from the New Testament gospels, which symbolizes the Hebrew conviction that this fearless man of unshakeable faith must have been especially dear to God. In the mystical vision known as the Transfiguration, the awe-stricken disciples saw two figures standing by the side of Jesus; they unhesitatingly identified them as Moses and Elijah.

V

THE GREAT PROPHETS

Elijah was not the only hero who emerged during the time of troubles through which Israel and Judah passed between the death of Solomon in 922 B.C., and the destruction of Jerusalem in 587 B.C. This turbulent era of intrigue, war, and apostasy also brought forth the great prophets Amos, Hosea, Isaiah, Micah, and Jeremiah. They are known as "writing prophets" because they used the medium of literature to communicate their message, in contrast with predecessors like Elijah and Nathan, who were "speaking prophets."

"The influence of the Hebrew prophets on human history has been so vast that it is impossible for any individual to appraise it or describe it," says Emil G. Kraeling, professor of Old Testament at Union Theological Seminary.

"Without the prophets there would have been no apostles and martyrs . . . all history would have been far different and far poorer."

The great prophets kept alive the true faith of Israel during a time when it was in serious danger of being submerged in a polytheistic culture. That alone would have been a sufficient achievement to put the whole human race in their debt. But they did not merely preserve the faith of their fathers. They strengthened and purified it. Their vision of what God is like, and what He requires of men, is the high-water mark of the Old Testament. You will not find more sublime spiritual insights except in the teachings of Jesus.

Much confusion about the prophets can be dispelled by understanding that foretelling the future was *not* their primary role. We tend today to think of a prophet as someone who goes around making predictions about what will happen tomorrow, or next week, or next year. The Hebrew prophets did occasionally forecast coming events, but they usually did so in the same spirit as a contemporary editorial writer or news commentator. That is, they pointed out the consequences that could logically be expected from certain courses of action.

The Hebrew word, *nabi,* which is translated "prophet" in English Bibles, has the connotation of "message bearer." The prophets were men called by God to serve as His messengers to a stubborn and unheeding people. They were always careful to point out that they were not voicing their own wisdom. Their warnings, entreaties and promises were always prefaced by the awesome proclamation:

"Thus says the Lord . . ."

When the prophets did engage in prognostication, they usually were concerned with events which were fairly close at hand, such as the Assyrian conquest of Israel and the Babylonian conquest of Judah (both of which they foretold with deadly accuracy). But occasionally a prophet's vision ranged farther into the future, to the day when God would enter into a new covenant with his rebellious children. The hope of reconciliation was often linked with the coming of a very particular person, a Messiah or Savior.

What made the prophets so sure that they had a right, nay a duty, to speak in the name of God? It is clear from their writings that they were not megalomaniacs who confused their own thoughts with the voice of God. On the contrary, they were humble men, awe-stricken by the responsibilities thrust upon them. Jeremiah tells how he shied away from the call to prophesy.

> Now the word of the Lord came to me saying,
> "Before I formed you in the womb I knew you,
>   and before you were born I consecrated you;
> I appointed you a prophet to the nations."
> Then I said, "Ah, Lord God! Behold, I do not know
>   how to speak,
>   for I am only a youth."
> But the Lord said to me,
> "Do not say, 'I am only a youth';
> for to all to whom I send you you shall go,
> and whatever I command you you shall speak.
> Be not afraid of them,
> For I am with you to deliver you."
>
> Jeremiah 1:4–10

All of the other prophets refer to some kind of mystical

or ecstatic experience in which they received their commission and their message. Isaiah's description of his call is magnificent poetic imagery:

> In the year that King Uzziah died I saw the Lord sitting upon a throne, high and lifted up; and his train filled the temple. Above him stood the seraphim; each had six wings: with two he covered his face, and with two he covered his feet, and with two he flew. And one called to another and said:

> > "Holy, holy, holy is the Lord of hosts;
> > the whole earth is full of his glory."

> And the foundations of the thresholds shook at the voice of him who called, and the house was filled with smoke. And I said: "Woe is me! For I am lost; for I am a man of unclean lips, and I dwell in the midst of a people of unclean lips; for my eyes have seen the King, the Lord of hosts!"

> Then flew one of the seraphim to me, having in his hand a burning coal which he had taken with tongs from the altar. And he touched my mouth, and said: "Behold, this has touched your lips; your guilt is taken away, and your sin forgiven."

> And I heard the voice of the Lord saying, "Whom shall I send, and who will go for us?" Then I said, "Here I am! Send me."

> > > Isaiah 6:1–8

A man who claimed that God had spoken to him was received then pretty much as he would be received now. Hosea records the skeptical reaction of his listeners:

> > The prophet is a fool,
> > The man of the spirit is mad.
> > > Hosea 9:7

The prophets minced no words in their indictments of the sins of Israel and Judah, and they trod especially hard on the toes of the rich, the powerful, and the pious. The Establishment responded then as some church members are wont to respond now when a preacher speaks out on controversial public issues:

"One should not preach of such things!"   (Micah 2:6)

The prophets were always unpopular, frequently banished, and sometimes persecuted. But it would not have occurred to them to buy acceptance at the price of soft-pedaling their message.

"The Lord God has spoken," explained Amos. "Who can but prophesy?"

It is no mean tribute to the Hebrew prophets that, after more than twenty-five centuries, their successors in the pulpits of the world still apply the admiring adjective "prophetic" to a sermon that is particularly relevant and courageous.

AMOS

The first of the great writing prophets was a shepherd named AMOS who thundered forth his warnings to the kingdom of Israel during the reign of Jeroboam II, between 786 and 746 B.C.

If you find Amos' words hitting very close to home, it is because he lived in an environment strikingly similar, in many respects, to contemporary America. Israel's foreign and domestic crises had not yet begun. It was enjoying a period of peace and prosperity, which many Israelites regarded as a sign of God's special favor. There were, to be sure, pockets of poverty in the affluent society. There was social injustice, discrimination, and exploitation of the weak. But the well-to-do had no sense of sin about this situation. They were regular in their attendance at the temple. They performed the prescribed rituals and paid their tithes. And they thought that was all God expected of them.

It was to this self-satisfied society that Amos spoke. And his words must have come as a great shock.

"Thus says the Lord to the house of Israel," said Amos:

"I hate, I despise your feasts,
    and I take no delight in your solemn assemblies.
Even though you offer me your burnt offerings and
    cereal offerings,
I will not accept them,
    and the peace offerings of your fatted beasts
I will not look upon.
Take away from me the noise of your songs;
    to the melody of your harps I will not listen.
But let justice roll down like waters,
    and righteousness like an ever-flowing stream."

                                        Amos 5:21–24

You can read the Book of Amos straight through. It's very short—only nine chapters. Chapter 1 and the first part of chapter 2 are devoted to "oracles"—that is, judgments and warnings—against Israel's neighbors, the cities of Damascus, Gaza, and Tyre, and the lands of Edom, Ammon, and Moab. You can almost hear the applause that these passages must have won from Amos' audience.

But in the sixth verse of the second chapter, the prophet suddenly turns his fire on his own people. Israel also has incurred the Lord's displeasure "because they sell the righteous for silver, and the needy for a pair of shoes." This was a reference to the custom of allowing poor people to be sold into slavery in payment for debts.

Amos also calls attention to a sharp decline in standards of sexual morality. Things have reached the point where "a man and his father go in to the same maiden"—that is, patronize the same prostitute.

And Israel's sins are particularly redolent because it is supposed to be a nation under God.

> Hear this word that the Lord has spoken against you, O people of Israel . . .
> "You only have I known of all the families of the earth;
> Therefore will I punish you for all your iniquities."

Amos 3:1-2

An annotated Bible is particularly valuable in reading the prophets, because it explains allusions that might otherwise mean nothing to you. But Amos does not really need extensive interpretation. It takes no great imagination, for example, to realize that it is Israel's suburban housewives whom he addresses irreverently as "you cows of Bashan."

Conspicuous consumption was anathema to Amos. Note the scorn he heaps upon people who have not only a winter house, but also a summer house; who insist on serving expensive spring lamb instead of thrifty mutton; and who furnish their homes extravagantly (the "beds of ivory" to which he refers were ivory-inlaid couches; archaeologists have found remains of them).

He also thought that there was entirely too much drinking in middle and upper class society. That's what he means when he pronounces "woe" upon those "who drink wine in bowls." (A temperate person would have been satisfied with a cup instead of a bowl.)

It is really not surprising that the high priest Amaziah

called Amos in and urged him to go down to Judah and preach to them for a while.

Prophets with a passion for social justice can be very annoying in any generation.

HOSEA

HOSEA also prophesied in the Northern Kingdom, a decade or two after Amos. Even in that short period of time, Israel had undergone a sharp decline from the era of peace and prosperity in which Amos preached. The armies of Assyria had begun to threaten Israel's existence, and the shakiness of the kingdom was reflected in great internal tension. The history of the period, recorded in the second book of Kings, shows that four kings were assassinated in fifteen years. Amos had spoken words of warning to a complacent people. Hosea came to offer assurances of God's love to a frightened and demoralized people.

Hosea's message was summed up in an allegory which he actually enacted in his own life. He married a whore. When his "wife of harlotry" betrayed him, he forgave her and took her back. This, Hosea said, is the way God deals with his people. Even when they are faithless and go astray, He is always ready to forgive them and take them back.

Nowhere outside the New Testament will you find such a strong sense of God's compassionate love as in the writing of Hosea.

Hosea does not gloss over the sins of Israel, any more than he fools himself about the conduct of his wife Gomer.

"There is no faithfulness or kindness, and no knowledge of God in the land," he says. "There is swearing, lying, killing, stealing, and committing adultery; they break all bounds and murder follows murder" (Hosea 4:1-2).

And God is not mocked. He will "punish them for their deeds."

But God's punishment, which will fall upon Israel, is not vengeful. It is corrective punishment, whose object is restoration and reconciliation.

> Come, let us return to the Lord;
> For he has torn, that he may heal us;
> He has stricken, and he will bind us up.
>
> Hosea 6:1

Compare Hosea's concept of God with the bloodthirsty tribal war-god of the period of the Judges, and you will be able to appreciate what a massive advance was represented by the religion of the prophets.

All fourteen chapters of the short book of Hosea are worth reading. But I particularly commend chapter 11, in which Hosea switches from his usual husband-wife metaphor to a father-son metaphor in describing God's relationship to Israel. The tenderness of this passage will be more readily apparent if you know that Ephraim was Joseph's son, and hence a symbol for all the children of Israel.

ISAIAH

The BOOK OF ISAIAH, as it appears in modern Bibles, is a composite of the writings of at least two and possibly three different prophets. At present, we will be concerned only with the first thirty-nine chapters, which are the work of Isaiah the son of Amoz, otherwise known as Isaiah of Jerusalem or the first Isaiah.

This Isaiah was the greatest of all the Hebrew prophets

and one of the greatest poets of all time. If you were able to read only one brief portion of the prophetic writings, I would unhesitatingly recommend that it be the first thirty-nine chapters of Isaiah.

Isaiah carried on his ministry in the kingdom of Judah between the years 742 and 687 B.C. This was the critical period during which the kingdom of Israel was swallowed up by the Assyrian Empire, and Judah maintained a precarious existence as a state only by paying tribute to the Assyrian Emperor.

Isaiah did not come from humble origins, like Amos and Hosea. He was an aristocrat, a wealthy landowner, a blood relative of the royal family. He did not have to issue his warnings from a distance. He could walk right into the palace and address the king to his face—as he very often did. He lived through the reigns of five kings, including one who was very wicked (Ahaz) and one who was quite a good man (Hezekiah). He was a statesman as well as a prophet, and he gave excellent foreign policy advice to Judah's kings. For example, he warned them not to rely on a military alliance with Egypt to save them from foreign aggressors. Unfortunately for Judah's future, Isaiah's advice was not often heeded. Some of Isaiah's involvements in statecraft are described in chapters 36 through 39.

But if Isaiah had done no more than advise the rulers of a tiny Middle Eastern kingdom which vanished more than 2500 years ago, there would be little point in our reading his words today. We revere Isaiah not because he was right about the Egyptians, but because he rose to greater heights than any other Old Testament author in his comprehension of the holiness and majesty of God.

Isaiah surpassed even his contemporary Amos in his passionate concern for social justice. He understood bet-

ter than any man before his time, and better than most
men since his time, that God cares nothing for the lip
service of ritualistic religion: He is concerned with how
men treat each other.

"What to me is the multitude of your sacrifices?"
    says the Lord;
"I have had enough of burnt offerings of rams
    and the fat of fed beasts;
I do not delight in the blood of bulls
    or of lambs, or of he-goats.

"When you come to appear before me,
    who requires of you
    this trampling of my courts?
Bring no more vain offerings;
    incense is an abomination to me.
New moon and sabbath and the calling of assemblies—
    I cannot endure iniquity and solemn assembly.
Your new moons and your appointed feasts
    my soul hates;
    they have become a burden to me,
    I am weary of bearing them.
When you spread forth your hands,
    I will hide my eyes from you;
    even though you make many prayers,
    I will not listen;
    your hands are full of blood.
Wash yourselves; make yourselves clean;
    remove the evil of your doings
    from before my eyes;
    cease to do evil,
    learn to do good;
seek justice,
    correct oppression;

defend the fatherless,
  plead for the widow."

Isaiah 1:11–17

For sheer power of language, Isaiah has no peer in the Old Testament and few rivals in the whole realm of literature. His poetry ranges like a great symphony orchestra from fortissimo to pianissimo, from fearsome accents of denunciation to idyllic visions of a future Messianic age.

Hear the blunt outrage with which the prophet speaks to the fat cats of Judean society:

"What do you mean by crushing my people,
    by grinding the face of the poor?"
  says the Lord God of hosts.

Isaiah 3:15

Listen to the contempt that drips from every word when Isaiah addresses the vain, materialistic women of Jerusalem:

Because the daughters of Zion are haughty
    and walk with outstretched necks,
    glancing wantonly with their eyes,
  mincing along as they go,
    tinkling with their feet;
  the Lord will smite with a scab
    the heads of the daughters of Zion,
    and the Lord will lay bare their secret parts.

Isaiah 3:16–17

And he is equally hard on the men of Jerusalem who are "heroes at drinking wine, valiant at mixing strong drink."

But if Isaiah can be as wrathful as Amos, he also can be as compassionate as Hosea. Isaiah's God demands righteousness. But He is always ready to forgive.

> Come now, let us reason together,
>   says the Lord:
> though your sins are like scarlet,
>   they shall be as white as snow;
> though they are red like crimson,
>   they shall become like wool.
>
> Isaiah 1:18

The most sublime passages of Isaiah's poetry are those in which he looks ahead to the coming of the Messiah. There are two poems in particular that have moved human hearts for twenty-five centuries. If translation is the ultimate test of poetry, we must stand in awe of these verses, which have been translated into more than a thousand tongues, from English to Urdu, without losing any of their power.

One of these poems you've doubtless heard at many Christmas services:

> For to us a child is born,
>   to us a son is given;
> and the government will be upon his shoulder,
>   and his name will be called
> "Wonderful Counselor, Mighty God,
>   Everlasting Father, Prince of Peace."
> Of the increase of his government and of peace
>   there will be no end,
> upon the throne of David, and over his kingdom,
>   to establish it, and to uphold it
> with justice and with righteousness
>   from this time forth and for evermore.
> The zeal of the Lord of hosts will do this.
>
> Isaiah 9:6–7

The other may be less familiar, but is even more beautiful:

There shall come forth a shoot
  from the stump of Jesse,
and a branch shall grow out of his roots.
And the Spirit of the Lord shall rest upon him,
  the spirit of wisdom and understanding,
  the spirit of counsel and might,
  the spirit of knowledge and the fear of the Lord.
And his delight shall be in the fear of the Lord.

He shall not judge by what his eyes see,
  or decide by what his ears hear;
but with righteousness he shall judge the poor,
  and decide with equity for the meek of the earth;
and he shall smite the earth with the rod of his mouth,
  and with the breath of his lips he shall slay the wicked.
Righteousness shall be the girdle of his waist,
  and faithfulness the girdle of his loins.

The wolf shall dwell with the lamb,
  and the leopard shall lie down with the kid,
and the calf and the lion and the fatling together,
  and a little child shall lead them.
The cow and the bear shall feed;
  their young shall lie down together;
  and the lion shall eat straw like the ox.
The sucking child shall play over the hole of the asp,
  and the weaned child shall put his hand on the adder's
    den.
They shall not hurt or destroy
  in all my holy mountain;
for the earth shall be full of the knowledge of the Lord
  as the waters cover the sea.

                                       Isaiah 11:1–9

MICAH

MICAH was a young contemporary of Isaiah. (The number of great prophets who emerged in one small country during this relatively brief period of history seems incredible until you remember that something very similar happened, in the realm of art, in the city of Florence during the early years of the Renaissance.)

Micah was no nobleman like Isaiah, but a man of the people from the little village of Moresheth in the foothills southwest of Jerusalem. He was shocked by the iniquity of the big city, and was the first prophet to forecast the destruction of Jerusalem (Micah 3:9–12). The seven chapters of his brief book are all worth reading, although as poetry they admittedly fall short of Isaiah's high standard. In at least one verse, which the late Adlai E. Stevenson called his favorite passage of Scripture, Micah achieves greatness:

> He has showed you, O man, what is good;
> and what does the Lord require of you
> but to do justice, and to love kindness,
> and to walk humbly with your God?
> Micah 6:8

JEREMIAH

Posterity has done a great injustice to JEREMIAH, by making his name a synonym for pessimist. Actually, Jeremiah was no handwringing doom-crier. The trait that really stands out from his writing is his unshakeable faith.

It is true that there are pessimistic passages in the long book that bears his name. But Jeremiah had abundant reason for occasional bouts of the blues. He prophesied during the darkest hours of Judah's history, from 627 B.C. until the final sack of Jerusalem in 587 B.C.

Jeremiah was born about 645 B.C., in the village of Anathoth, three miles north of Jerusalem. He came from a wealthy upper-class family: one of his ancestors was David's high priest, Abiathar. His call to prophesy came when he was a youth of nineteen, and is recorded in the first chapter of the book which he dictated to a scribe named Baruch.*

Like Isaiah, Jeremiah was deeply concerned with practical questions of foreign policy. He offered sound advice to six successive kings, and for his pains was rewarded with public humiliation, imprisonment, and exile. His contempt for the weak and inglorious monarchs who ruled over Judah comes through quite clearly in his writing, and there is no reason to think that Jeremiah was any more tactful in expressing his opinions verbally at court. He was an abrasively honest man.

You don't need to read all fifty-two chapters of this very long and repetitious book. The latter chapters are so closely oriented to events of Judah's history that the contemporary reader needs a detailed commentary to make much sense of them. But there are pearls of great price in the first twenty-five chapters, which are an anthology of Jeremiah's speeches, sermons, poems, and oracles. And chapter 31 contains a lovely poem which looks forward to brighter days, when God will "make a new covenant" with his people and "remember their sin no more."

Like Hosea and Isaiah, Jeremiah emphasizes God's eagerness to be reconciled with his wayward people.

---

* Jeremiah is the only prophet who refers to the method of literary composition he used, which most if not all the other prophets must have employed. See Jeremiah 36:1-4.

"Return, faithless Israel,"
                    says the Lord;
"I will not look on you in anger
    for I am merciful,"
                    says the Lord;
"I will not be angry for ever."
                    Jeremiah 3:12

But reconciliation can come only when the Israelites acknowledge that they have rebelled against God and have fallen into wicked ways. Jeremiah does his best to make them see how depraved they have become:

Run to and fro through the streets of Jerusalem,
    look and take note!
Search her squares to see
    if you can find a man,
one who does justice
    and seeks truth . . .

                    Jeremiah 5:1

Jeremiah's literary style is often tedious. But he has his moments, when a vivid metaphor flashes brightly across the page. Hear his characterization of Jerusalem's adulterous husbands:

They are well-fed lusty stallions,
    each neighing for his neighbor's wife.
                    Jeremiah 5:8

Also, his plaintive cry of near despair:

Is there no balm in Gilead?
Is there no physician there?
                    Jeremiah 8:22

By far the most interesting passages, however, are those in which Jeremiah records his own inner spiritual turmoil. He is the only one of the great prophets who shares with us his dark moments of doubt and torment, as well as his bright hours of faith and vision.

In chapter 12, we see the prophet wrestling with a question that has troubled many good men: "Why does the way of the wicked prosper?" In earlier parts of the Old Testament, we encountered a naïve kind of religion which insisted that good men were always rewarded and wicked men were always punished. But Jeremiah has moved beyond that. He knows that it is quite often just the other way around: those who try to do right suffer, while those who ignore God seem to have everything going their way. He does not understand why this should be. But it is a measure of his faith that he does not push the whole thing out of mind, as something that mustn't be thought about. Instead, he openly complains to God. And even as he complains, he acknowledges that there must be some explanation which he cannot yet fathom, for "righteous art thou, O Lord."

In 15:10–15 is an even more poignant personal lament, in which Jeremiah's despondency reaches the point of cursing the day that he was born. His fervent prayer in verse 15—"Take vengeance for me on my persecutors"— is a reminder that even the noblest of the Old Testament prophets never reached the heights of the Galilean teacher who, when he was hanging in agony on a cross, cried out, "Father, forgive them, for they know not what they do!"

In chapter 20 (verses 7 through 18), Jeremiah goes so far as to accuse God of deceiving him. And he again curses the day on which he was born.

> Why did I come forth from the womb
> to see toil and sorrow,
> and spend my days in shame?

Jeremiah's outcries against God sound almost blasphemous at times. But they are the protests of a man who loves God so much, and who is so certain of God's righteousness, that he can afford to quarrel with Him.

"Jeremiah bears the distinction of the first among the prophets to record his innermost experiences and as the first also to express the possible heights and depths of intimate communion with God," says Mary Ellen Chase, the great teacher who brought the Bible to life for students at Smith College. "In the midst of days of darkness and chaos, of despair, dejection and failure, of mental anguish, and even of anger against the life demanded of him, Jeremiah was able to preserve a tenacious and even an exultant faith. He was an ancient St. John of the Cross, who never doubted there was light even though it was invisible and who, in the days when his doomed world was falling about him, foreshadowed in moments of agony as well as illumination the dawning of a brighter day."

SECOND ISAIAH

After the Jews were carried away to Babylon, where they were destined to live in captivity for nearly half a century, another great writing prophet arose. You will find his work in chapters 40 through 55 of the Book of Isaiah. We don't know his real name. Scholars call him "Second Isaiah" or "Deutero-Isaiah," which means the same thing but sounds more impressive.

Although he gives us no autobiography, there are definite clues in his poetry to the kind of person he must have been. Isaiah II was a man of unquenchable faith and optimism. Living as a slave in exile, he was able to look ahead to a day of reconciliation, when God would gather up his scattered people as a shepherd gathers a lost lamb to his bosom.

Before the fall of the nation, the voice of prophecy had been characterized by an ominous tone of warning. Now that the disaster has taken place, there is a striking shift. Isaiah II makes clear in the opening words of chapter 40 that his mission is not to scold a stiffnecked nation, but to reassure a demoralized band of captives.

> Comfort, comfort my people,
>> says your God.
> Speak tenderly to Jerusalem,
>> and cry to her
> that her warfare is ended,
>> that her iniquity is pardoned,
> that she has received from the Lord's hand
>> double for all her sins.
>
> Isaiah 40:1–2

Isaiah II accurately forecast the release of the Jews from Babylonian captivity. There is an exultant note in his poetry, a sublime confidence in the sheltering goodness and mercy of God.

> He will feed his flock like a shepherd,
> He will gather the lambs in his arms,
> He will carry them in his bosom,
>> and gently lead those that are with young.
>
> Isaiah 40:11

He also rises to heights unequaled by any other prophet in his comprehension of God as the creator and sustainer of the cosmos.

> Who has measured the waters in the hollow of his hand
>> and marked off the heavens with a span,

enclosed the dust of the earth in a measure
  and weighed the mountains in scales
  and the hills in a balance?

Isaiah 40:12

President John F. Kennedy loved to quote one of the lyric passages in which Isaiah II voices his faith in the sustaining presence of God:

He gives power to the faint,
  and to him who has no might he increases strength.
Even youths shall faint and be weary,
  and young men shall fall exhausted;
but they who wait for the Lord shall renew their strength,
  they shall mount up with wings like eagles,
they shall run and not be weary,
  they shall walk and not faint.

Isaiah 40:29–31

Isaiah II also was a favorite of another young man, who like Kennedy was cut down in the prime of life. Jesus quoted often from this book of prophecy, and his understanding of his own ministry was clearly influenced by the image of the Suffering Servant which he found in the writings of the second Isaiah.

When you read these sixteen chapters, you will want to pay particular attention to the "Servant" passages which meant so much to Jesus. There are four of them: the first four verses of chapter 42; the first six of chapter 49; verses 4 through 9 of chapter 50; and the whole of chapter 53. Many scholars believe that Isaiah II was thinking of the whole nation of Israel, rather than a particular individual, as the Servant whose suffering benefits all mankind. It is improbable that the prophet consciously thought of these passages as descriptions of the future Messiah, whose role was envisioned as kingly. But what Isaiah II thought he was writing about is somewhat beside the point. What matters is that Jesus, reading this scripture five centuries later, saw in it a concept of the Messiah's role that was vastly different from Jewish expectations. If we take seriously the humanity of Jesus, and if we believe that God speaks to men through the Bible, there is no reason to boggle at the idea that Jesus' insight into His mission was deepened by what he read in Isaiah II. Certainly, when we read them today, some of the Suffering Servant passages read as though they were a description of Jesus written by an eyewitness after His crucifixion, rather than an exiled prophet's vision, set down 500 years before Jesus was born.

He was despised and rejected by men;
a man of sorrows and acquainted with grief;
and as one from whom men hide their faces
    he was despised, and we esteemed him not.

Surely he has borne our griefs
    and carried our sorrows;
yet we esteemed him stricken,
    smitten by God, and afflicted.
But he was wounded for our transgressions,
    he was bruised for our iniquities;
upon him was the chastisement that made us whole,
    and with his stripes we are healed.
All we like sheep have gone astray;
    we have turned every one to his own way;
and the Lord has laid on him
    the iniquity of us all.

Isaiah 53:3–6

OTHER BOOKS
OF HISTORY AND PROPHECY

The period of Babylonian captivity lasted from 587 to 538 B.C. The shifting tides of empire brought a new ruler to the fore in the Middle East. Cyrus, king of Persia, conquered Babylon in 539 B.C. Cyrus was one of history's most enlightened monarchs. He permitted the Jews to return to their homeland and to rebuild the temple in Jerusalem. The story of this "second exodus" and the rebuilding of Jerusalem is told in the books of EZRA and NEHEMIAH.

Jerusalem and its Judean environs remained under Persian rule for about two centuries. In 332 B.C., Alexander the Great gained control of Palestine on his way to conquer Egypt. After Alexander's death in 323 B.C., his Hellenistic empire was divided among his generals, and Judah was included in the parcel governed from Egypt by Ptolemy and his successors. In 198 B.C. a Syrian king, Seleucid Antiochus IV, extended his rule over Judah, and tried to force the Jews to adopt Greek ways and worship Greek gods.

Among other things, this despot converted the temple of Jerusalem into a shrine to Zeus. In 166 B.C., the long-suffering Jews finally rose in rebellion. Their heroic and successful struggle for independence is recounted in two books of the Old Testament Apocrypha, FIRST and SECOND MACCABEES. (They get their names from Judas Maccabeus and his family, the leaders of the uprising.) The temple was purified in 164 B.C., and rededicated to the worship of God—an event that is still commemorated by devout Jews in the annual celebration of the festival of Hanukkah, which falls near Christmas.

The independent Jewish state founded by the Maccabees endured until the arrival of Pompey's Roman legions in 63 B.C. Palestine remained a Roman protectorate until 40 B.C., when it lost even the semblance of independence it had so far been allowed to keep and was reduced to the status of an imperial province, governed by a crafty and ruthless Roman legate named Herod. You remember him—this is where you came in, when you began reading the New Testament book of Luke.

If you have developed a passionate interest in the details of Jewish history, by all means read Ezra, Nehemiah, and Maccabees. Otherwise, you can pass them by without irreparable loss.

You also will find in the Old Testament nine books of prophecy other than those mentioned above. One of them is a very long book (forty-eight chapters) by a priest named Ezekiel who ministered to the Jews during the Babylonian captivity. Perhaps you should sample Ezekiel. You may like him. Personally, I find him a rather dry and dour fellow, and I cannot bring myself to insist that you include him in your reading itinerary, at least on your first trip through the Bible. And the same goes for Joel, Obadiah, Nahum, Habakkuk, Zephaniah, Haggai, Zechariah, and Malachi.

VI

THE STIRRING NARRATIVES

Israel produced great writers of prose, as well as great poets. Some of the stirring narratives in the Old Testament are obviously meant to convey a "moral." But others seem to have been preserved mainly, if not entirely, for their entertainment value. And even those which have a message are so skillfully written that you may not realize, while you're absorbed in the author's tale, that he is concerned with promoting a point of view.

JONAH

The BOOK OF JONAH, only four chapters long, is a literary gem. Its message is that God loves all His creatures—"foreigners" as well as Members of the Club. The Jews needed to be reminded of this occasionally, as do Christians today. But the author of this little masterpiece never labors his point. He lets it emerge unobtrusively from his imaginative story of a recalcitrant prophet who balks at God's command that he preach to the foreigners of Nineveh, capital of the hated Assyrian Empire.

The unknown author wrote about the third century B.C., but his story is set 500 years earlier, during the reign of Jeroboam II (786–746 B.C.). The main character, Jonah, is based on a real prophet who is mentioned briefly in 2 Kings 14:25. But it is obvious that this story is not meant to be read as literal history, any more than are Jesus' parables.

The first of Jonah's adventures is familiar to everyone who was exposed in childhood to "Bible stories." Fleeing from God's presence, Jonah takes a ship at Joppa for distant Tarshish (probably Sardinia). But God sends a great storm that threatens to swamp the ship. The sailors learn by casting lots that the cause of their troubles is their cringing passenger, Jonah. (You will recognize here the origin of the ancient expression, "a Jonah," to denote one who seems to attract misfortune.) Jonah is heaved overboard and is swallowed by "a great fish" (the original text doesn't say it was a whale: that was a conclusion of mediaeval translators). Jonah prays for deliverance after three days and nights in the fish's belly, and his prayer is granted. "The Lord spoke to the fish, and it vomited out Jonah upon the dry land."

The last two chapters of the book, much less familiar to the average person, are really the richest part of the story. Here the author displays an urbane talent for satire. Jonah preaches to the sinners of Nineveh, but when they heed his words and repent, he is quite irritated! He had counted on seeing God rain destruction on these wicked people, and he is put out when God mercifully forgives them instead. There is a delightful passage in chapter 4 in which the author credits God with having a sense of humor, and depicts Him as teasing Jonah with a shade plant. The story ends with God patiently trying to explain to Jonah why He took pity on a city in which there were 120,000 innocent children, not to mention innocent beasts who would have perished in the rain of fire and brimstone that Jonah had hoped to see.

DANIEL

The BOOK OF DANIEL is sometimes listed among the books of prophecy, but this is a misleading category in which to place it. The last six chapters of the book are dream-visions which properly belong to the literary genre known as Apocalypse (which we discussed, you remember, in connection with the Book of Revelation. See page 116).

Most interesting to the modern reader are the first six chapters, which contain a series of fascinating narratives about a young Jew named Daniel who was one of those carried into Babylonian captivity by King Nebuchadnezzar. Daniel had three friends whose names have been immortalized by a great Negro spiritual, "Shadrach, Meshach, and Abednego."

The first story in the cycle is dear to the hearts of mothers and Sunday School teachers who have been using it for uncounted generations to persuade children that it pays to eat your vegetables and avoid alcoholic beverages. I'm sure you'll recognize it when you read it.

Equally familiar is the story of the fiery furnace in chapter 3. The author was mercifully spared from the knowledge that a day would come when some people would, in the name of piety, read his words literally. So he did not hesitate to pull out all the stops in constructing his parable of the triumph of faith over persecution. Thus we have old Nebuchadnezzar, "full of fury," ordering the furnace "heated seven times more than it was wont to be heated." It got so hot, in fact, that the guards who threw Shadrach, Meshach, and Abednego into the furnace were themselves burned up by the flames belching from the open door. But the faithful servants of God emerged from the trial by fire totally unharmed. In a particularly fine touch, the author says that they didn't even smell of smoke when they came out of the furnace.

In chapter 5, you will learn why we speak of a portent of doom as "the handwriting on the wall." And in chapter 6, Daniel is cast into the lion's den. (The king kept a lot of lions around because his favorite sport—attested by secular historical records of the era—was hunting lions from a chariot.)

RUTH

The German poet Goethe called the BOOK OF RUTH "the most beautiful of all idylls."

It was probably written about 450 B.C., after the return from Babylon. But, like a modern historical novel, it deals with a much earlier period of time. Its setting is the period of the Judges, about 1100 B.C. We have no clue to the author's identity, but we can deduce from what he has written that he was a liberal-minded man, who took a dim view of the drastic restrictions on mixed marriages which were imposed by Nehemiah and other Jewish leaders after the return from Babylon.

The essential point of the story is that Ruth, the heroine, was a Moabitess—one of the "foreign women" who were looked upon with such bitter suspicion and hostility during this era of intense Jewish nationalism. Without mounting a soapbox, the author preaches a highly effective sermon against chauvinism.

It's a charming story and requires no further commentary or interpretation. It's very brief and you can read it straight through in a few minutes.

ESTHER

The BOOK OF ESTHER is an historical novelette. The action takes place not in Palestine, but in Susa, the capital of the Persian Empire between 468 and 465 B.C., during the reign of Xerxes the Great (who is referred to in the Bible as Ahasuerus). Xerxes was the absolute master of the greatest empire the world had ever known up to that time, stretching all the way from India to Ethiopia. Among the subjects living in his capital were thousands of Jews who had chosen to continue living in Persia rather than return to Palestine. One of them was a "beautiful and lovely maiden" whose Hebrew name was Hadassah. She had attained marriageable age—about fourteen or fifteen. At the advice of her guardian Mordecai, who figured she'd go farther with a Persian name, she changed her name to Esther, which is the Persian word for "star."

How Esther gets into the King's harem, and eventually becomes his favorite wife, is vividly recounted in the Biblical text. The plot thickens when the villainous Prime Minister Haman—a spiritual forebear of Adolf Hitler—decides to conduct a nationwide pogrom to exterminate the Jews. Does Queen Esther outwit Haman and save her people? Read the story and see for yourself why she is the heroine of the Jewish festival of Purim, which is still celebrated annually.

Although Esther is a more dramatic narrative than Ruth, it represents a much lower level of spiritual insight. The characters in Esther are a pretty crummy lot, not excluding the Queen herself, who aside from one brave deed was largely concerned with looking out for Number One. And the story closes on a note of brutal vengeance, as the Jews who are saved from slaughter retaliate by murdering 75,510 Gentiles whom they disliked.

Because it panders to the basest sentiments of chauvinism, and because it is virtually devoid of any distinctive Jewish religious ideas (the name of God is not mentioned once in the entire book), Esther was long a bone of contention among Jewish scholars, with many rabbis contending that it had no place in the canon of Scripture. Even today, it is generally agreed by Jewish and Christian scholars that this is not a particularly edifying segment of the Bible.

SUSANNA

The one-chapter book of SUSANNA is part of the Old Testament Apocrypha and is sufficient reason by itself for buying a Bible which includes the Apocrypha. It is perhaps the earliest forerunner of the modern detective story, and its basic plot is still being used in contemporary whodunits.

Susanna was a virtuous wife who was falsely accused of adultery by two suitors whom she had spurned. In a courtroom scene that Agatha Christie has never surpassed, Susanna is saved from condemnation by a brilliant piece of detection on the part of a young judge named

Daniel—the same fellow you encountered in the Book of Daniel. And that's enough introduction: if I say any more I'll spoil the plot.

JUDITH

If Susanna foreshadows the modern detective story, the BOOK OF JUDITH, which also is found in the Apocrypha, may be considered a prototype of the spy novel. It is written with a brutal realism that would do credit to Ian Fleming or John Le Carré, and it builds toward what one commentator has aptly called "a climax of unforgettable horror."

The heroine, Judith, is depicted as a pious and patriotic Jewish widow who lived during the time of troubles, just before the fall of Judah, when the armies of Nebuchadnezzar were laying waste the land. You can skip lightly over the first seven chapters, which are intended only to lay the groundwork for the story by describing the relentless advance of the Babylonian forces under command of General Holofernes. The story really begins in chapter 8, when Judith is introduced. The rest of the book is taken up with hair-raising details of her daring mission as a secret agent who not only penetrates the enemy's lines, but even makes her way into Holofernes' bed. Sex, it seems, was a major ingredient of successful cloak-and-dagger work long before James Bond.

TOBIT

Another book of the Apocrypha which is worthy of your attention is TOBIT. Bruce M. Metzger calls it "a fascinating amalgam of *Arabian Nights* romance, kindly Jewish piety, and sound moral teaching." It was probably written during the second century B.C., but some of the folklore which it contains may have circulated in Israel long before that.

The best part of the book is the tender love story of Tobit's son, Tobias, and a girl named Sarah who had acquired rather a bad name among young men of the country because she had had seven husbands, all of whom had died violently on their wedding nights. It turns out that a demon named Asmodeus is in love with Sarah and is killing off her husbands to keep her for himself. Tobias' guardian angel, Raphael, saves the day, and the young lovers live happily ever after.

VII

WISDOM LITERATURE

It is evident from numerous references in the Old Testament that Israel recognized three distinct types of religious teachers. There were *priests,* who conducted religious ceremonies and interpreted the Mosaic law. There were *prophets,* who spoke with great immediacy the Word of God as they had heard it for their own time. And there were *wise men,* who served at court as royal counselors or conducted schools for the instruction of the young.

Like the priests and the prophets, the wise men made a large contribution to the Hebrew scriptures. Their writings are known, appropriately, as *wisdom literature.*

Most and probably all of the wisdom literature which has been preserved in the Old Testament and the Apocrypha was written down, in its present form, after the Jews returned from Babylonian exile in the sixth century B.C. But these postexilic books were comparable to modern anthologies. They included material from many different sources and many different eras of history.

It was customary for the editor of a wisdom book to attribute its authorship to Solomon. This is purely a literary convention, and reflects Solomon's traditional status as the patron saint of Hebrew wisdom. We are told by Solomon's rather sycophantic biographer (in 1 Kings 4:29–34) that "the wisest man who ever lived" composed 3000 proverbs and 1005 songs, and it is certainly possible that some of his sayings have been included in the books ascribed to his authorship. But we can tell from language, concepts, allusions to events, and other internal dating clues that much of the material in these books had to originate centuries after Solomon's death. That Solomonic authorship of the wisdom books is not meant to be taken literally is most plainly evident in the Apocryphal book known as the Wisdom of Solomon, which was written *in Greek* about 50 B.C.

Some Biblical commentators feel that the practical moral precepts expounded in wisdom literature are a sharp comedown from the lofty spiritual plane attained by the prophets. Mary Ellen Chase, for example, observes that the wise men seem to have been concerned primarily with "getting on successfully in life."

"Their motives are always those leading to personal security and happiness," she says. "There is little in their teaching that concerns the welfare of others. Kindness brings a reward; therefore it is better than unkindness."

R. B. Y. Scott of Princeton University, a leading authority on wisdom literature, agrees that some of the Hebrew proverbs preserved in the Bible are "simply observations on life and experience, without much positive moral content."* It also is true that the wise men have almost nothing to say about institutional religion, which was the great concern of the priests, and they rarely mention the special relationship between God and Israel, which was the passionate interest of the prophets.

"The wise men and their writings were a kind of 'third force' in religious and social life of the people of the Old Testament," says Scott. "They make no direct appeal to the authority of a revealed religion, though their occasional exhortations to piety presuppose an accepted belief in God. The authority to which they chiefly appeal is the disciplined intelligence and moral experience of good men."

But the pragmatic tone of wisdom literature does not mean that it is devoid of spiritual content, Scott emphasizes. Even at its most mundane level, Hebrew wisdom was informed by a profound belief in the sovereignty of God. It sought to spell out "a practical religious philosophy through which a good man might find satisfaction in life."

My personal view, which I hesitate to intrude on a topic so thoroughly canvassed by experts, is that wisdom literature has precisely the characteristic one would expect to find in an anthology: namely, variety. Some of the sayings are witty; others are sententious. Their observations about life range from trite to profound. And the moral level of their counsel covers the whole gamut from self-regarding prudence to an almost Christ-like generosity of

* This and the following quotations from R. B. Y. Scott are from the Introduction to *Proverbs. Ecclesiastes* (The Anchor Bible, 18; New York, 1965).

spirit. This is a part of the Bible in which it is particularly necessary for the reader to use discrimination—in short, to apply a little of his own wisdom—in separating the wheat from the chaff. If you approach these books in that spirit, I think you'll find them quite a helpful source of light for your daily pathway.

PROVERBS

The BOOK OF PROVERBS is the best place to begin your sampling of wisdom literature. It is the most typical of all the wisdom books, displaying all of the strengths and weaknesses of the genre.

Webster's New World Dictionary defines a proverb as "a short saying in common use that strikingly expresses some obvious truth or familiar experience." That definition probably comes pretty close to the meaning which the word has for the average modern reader. But the Hebrew word *māshāl*, which is translated "proverb" in English Bibles, has a much broader connotation. It can be applied to any brief didactic saying which attempts to express a truth about the human condition.

The traditional literary form for Hebrew proverbs was the "thought-rhymed" couplet—two lines of poetry expressing the same idea in different words. Sometimes the relation between the first and second line is that of contrast:

> The wicked flee when no one pursues,
> But the righteous are bold as a lion.
> > Proverbs 28:1

In another variation, the second line of the couplet explains or completes the thought of the first line:

Let your foot be seldom in your neighbor's house,
Lest he become weary of you and hate you.

Proverbs 25:17

Train up a child in the way he should go,
And when he is old he will not depart from it.

Proverbs 22:6

You may find it an interesting exercise, while reading Proverbs, to jot down in the margin a running list of all the virtues which are commended and all of the vices which are condemned.

You will find that Hebrew wise men attached great importance to hard work, and conversely, looked with horror upon laziness.

Go to the ant, O sluggard;
consider her ways, and be wise.
Without having any chief,
officer or ruler,
she prepares her food in summer,
and gathers her sustenance in harvest.
How long will you lie there, O sluggard?
When will you arise from your sleep?
A little sleep, a little slumber,
a little folding of the hands to rest,
and poverty will come upon you like a vagabond,
and want like an armed man.

Proverbs 6:6–11

They took a dim view of philandering:

Drink water from your own cistern . . . He who commits adultery has no sense.

Proverbs 5:15; 6:32

And also of drunkenness:

> Do not look at wine when it is red (i.e., undiluted)
> When it sparkles in the cup
>   and goes down smoothly.
> At the last it bites like a serpent
>   and stings like an adder.
>
> Proverbs 23:31–32

They felt strongly that domestic strife was a thing to be avoided:

> It is better to live in a corner of the housetop,
>   than in a palace shared with a contentious woman.
>
> Proverbs 21:9

> Better is a dry morsel with quiet,
>   than a house full of feasting with strife.
>
> Proverbs 17:1

> Better is a dinner of herbs where love is,
>   than a fatted ox and hatred with it.
>
> Proverbs 15:17

Although the wise men were not as impassioned as the prophets in their concern for social justice, they cannot fairly be accused of ignoring the problems of the poor. Some of their comments are sardonic:

> The poor is disliked even by his neighbor,
>   but the rich has many friends.
>
> Proverbs 14:20

But at other times, they drop the pose of witty sophistication and speak almost as bluntly as a prophet:

> He who oppresses a poor man
>   insults his Maker.

> But he who is kind to the needy,
>> honors God.
>>> Proverbs 14:31

The temptation to go on quoting from Proverbs is very great, but must be resisted lest you conclude that there's no need in your exploring this treasure house for yourself. I recommend that you read the whole book of Proverbs, limiting yourself to one chapter at a sitting. Women will be particularly interested in the description of the Ideal Housewife in the last chapter (Proverbs 31:10–31). Familiarity with this passage once was regarded as part of a young girl's preparation for marriage.

SIRACH
(ALSO KNOWN AS ECCLESIASTICUS)

My personal favorite among the wisdom books is found in the Apocrypha. Its full title is the Wisdom of Jesus the Son of Sirach, or SIRACH for short. During the third century A.D., it came to be known in the Latin Church as Ecclesiasticus, which means "the Church Book." Catholics still know it by this name.

The author was a Jewish scribe who conducted an academy for the sons of well-to-do families in Jerusalem. The book contains his lectures, admonitions, and instructions to the young men placed in his charge. It was written about 180 B.C.

Sirach's philosophy is less pragmatic and more deeply infused with religious faith than the general run of wisdom literature. Time and again, you will find that his counsel is fully as applicable to an adult of the twentieth century A.D. as to a youth of the second century B.C.

For example, consider his advice about humiliation:

Accept whatever is brought upon you,
   and in changes that humble you, be patient.
For gold is tested in the fire,
   and acceptable men in the furnace of humiliation.

                              Sirach 2:4–5

At times, Sirach sounds very much like Jesus:

The greater you are, the more you must humble yourself;
   so you will find favor in the sight of the Lord.

                              Sirach 3:18

    Forgive your neighbor the wrong he has done,
       and then your sins will be pardoned
          when you pray.

                          Sirach 28:2

Sirach's advice about practical problems often has a warmly personal touch to it, which suggests that he is speaking from firsthand experience. One of his finest passages has to do with choosing and keeping friends.

When you gain a friend, gain him through testing,
   and do not trust him hastily,
For there is a friend who is such
   at his own convenience
But will not stand by you in your day of trouble . . .
A faithful friend, however, is a sturdy shelter:
   he that has found one has found a treasure.
There is nothing so precious as a faithful friend,
   and no scales can measure his excellence.

                           Sirach 6:7–15

He must have been a happily married man, for he counsels a young man:

Do not deprive yourself of a wise and good wife,
    for her charm is worth more than gold.
                                Sirach 7:19

We can also deduce that he had a teen-age daughter. He is surely not speaking from hearsay when he reports:

A daughter keeps her father secretly wakeful,
    and worry over her robs him of sleep;
when she is young, lest she do not marry,
    or if married, lest she be hated;
while a virgin, he worries lest she be defiled,
    or become pregnant in her father's house;
    or having a husband, lest she prove unfaithful,
    or though married, lest she be barren.
Keep strict watch over a headstrong daughter,
    lest she make you a laughingstock to your enemies,
    a byword in the city and notorious among the people
    and put you to shame before the great multitude.
                         Sirach 42:9–11

Sirach had no sympathy for aging males who feel a compulsion to demonstrate their virility.

My soul hates three kinds of men,
And I am greatly offended at their life:
    A beggar who is proud, a rich man who is a liar,
    And an adulterous old man who lacks good sense.
                          Sirach 25:2

He liked his glass of wine, but was a great believer in moderation:

      Wine is like life to men,
        If you drink it in moderation.
      What is life to man who is without wine?
        It has been created to make men glad.

Wine drunk in season and temperately
   is rejoicing of heart and gladness of soul.
Wine drunk to excess is bitterness of soul,
   with provocation and stumbling.
Drunkenness increases the anger of a fool to his injury,
   reducing his strength and adding wounds.

                                        Sirach 31:27–30

The Book of Sirach or Ecclesiasticus is fifty-one chapters
long. While the literary quality is uneven, there is, in my
opinion, more than enough sustenance to warrant your
reading the first forty-three chapters in their entirety. I
won't argue for the last eight, which are devoted to a
recitation of the deeds of Israel's great heroes, and which
probably constituted the history course at the Sirach
Academy.

THE SONG OF SOLOMON

It is very difficult sometimes to comprehend the rea-
soning of the men who decided which books should be
included in the Hebrew canon of Old Testament scripture. We find a truly great book like Sirach relegated to
the Apocrypha; and squarely among the wisdom books
which were accorded canonical status we find the SONG
OF SOLOMON.

This is a short anthology of love poems, such as might
have been recited at weddings. They are sensuous, even
erotic, in imagery, and their inclusion in Holy Writ was
a source of extreme embarrassment to our Puritan fore-
fathers. In an effort to explain how this sexy poetry found
its way into the Bible, Jewish scholars have traditionally
interpreted the Song as an allegory of God's love for
Israel. Christian scholars, not to be outdone in exegetical
acrobatics, have called it an allegory of the Church as the

Bride of Christ. Plain common sense balks at both of these explanations. As any reader can see who approaches it with an open mind, this lyric verse was never meant to be weighed down with allegorical meaning. It is an earthy, uninhibited celebration of the joys of physical sex as part of God's good creation.

One sample should suffice to prove the point:

> How fair and pleasant you are,
> O loved one, delectable maiden,
> You are stately as a palm tree,
>   and your breasts are like its clusters,
> I say I will climb the palm tree
>   and lay hold of its branches.
>   Song of Solomon 7:6-8

This comparatively brief book (it has only eight chapters) has been a heavily mined source of titles for novels and plays. See how many you can spot.

ECCLESIASTES

If the inclusion of the Song of Solomon in the Old Testament canon is perplexing, the decision in favor of EC-CLESIASTES is totally inexplicable. This book was written by an agnostic who flatly rejected all of Israel's basic religious beliefs. He expounds the futility of all human effort ("All is vanity"), and says that the only "good" is to enjoy life as much as possible. The only conceivable explanation for the inclusion of this book in the Old Testament is that some Biblical literalists of long ago took seriously the author's tongue-in-cheek attribution of his work to Solomon. If you decide to read it, do so in the realization that this is not an expression of Hebrew religion, but of a rationalist Greek philosophy (possibly a type of Epicureanism) which arrived in Palestine, along with other aspects of Hellenist culture, in the baggage of Alexander the Great. If you're already familiar with the cynical view that life is essentially meaningless, you can skip this book without missing a thing.

JOB

The BOOK OF JOB is traditionally included in the category of "wisdom literature." But it really belongs in a class by itself. "There is nothing quite like it either in the Old Testament or in any other literature," says Marvin Pope of Yale University. Job is a profound exploration of a theological question that has troubled thoughtful men and women of every age, and is still very much alive today. Theologians call it "the problem of evil." It can be summarized in a few words:

Why does God permit innocent people to suffer?

The question has a sharp point because Jews and Christians have always asserted two things about God: first, that He is all-powerful; and second, that He is righteous and merciful. It is easy enough to find a solution to the problem of evil if you are prepared to deny either God's omnipotence or His love. But if you insist on both of these attributes—as Biblical religion emphatically does—you are confronted with a quandary to which there is no nice, pat, logical answer.

There is, however, a way of begging the question. You can close your eyes to the plain evidence of everyday life and deny that the innocent sometimes suffer (or conversely, that the wicked sometimes prosper). This is what most pious Jews did before Job came along. Even in the parts of the Old Testament which otherwise achieve the highest levels of spiritual insight—the writings of the great prophets and the Psalms—you find the reiterated theme that God always rewards the righteous and punishes the wicked, right here in this earthly life.

"Fret not yourself because of the wicked," says the author of Psalm 37. "For the wicked shall be cut off; but those who wait for the Lord shall possess the land."

Before the time of Job, the one concession Hebrew piety was able to make was this: God would sometimes permit misfortunes to befall those He loves, to correct their ways, strengthen their character, or test their faith.

Job directly challenges this whole outlook. It raises the problem of evil in the most acute form imaginable: no agnostic could possibly put the question more searchingly than this extraordinary book does.

The main character of the story, Job, is introduced in the very first sentence as a man "blameless and upright, one who feared God, and turned away from evil." As the story opens, he is enjoying great prosperity, just as Hebrew orthodoxy promised for such a person. But his fortunes suddenly turn sour. Every conceivable disaster descends upon him, and he becomes so despondent that he fervently curses the day he was born.

Pope, the author of the superb translation of Job for the Anchor Bible series, points out the absurdity of speaking (as our Biblically literate forebears were wont to do) of "the patience of Job." Far from being patient under his afflictions, Job protests them in near-blasphemous tirades against God. He flatly accuses God of being unjust. All of us have dark moments in which we feel like making that accusation, but few of us are honest enough to come right out and say it.

Three friends come to console Job in his troubles. How little help they were is reflected in the sardonic meaning which long usage has attached to the phrase, "Job's comforters."

The "comforters"—Eliphaz, Bildad, and Zophar—confront poor old Job with a seemingly irrefutable syllogism in which the main premise is the hitherto-unchallenged doctrine of exact individual retribution. "Only the wicked suffer," they assure Job. "You are suffering. Therefore, you must have done something wrong. Why don't you come clean and admit it?"

But Job steadfastly insists: "I am blameless." And he bluntly challenges God to meet him face to face and tell him just what he has done to deserve all this trouble:

> Behold, he will slay me; I have no hope.
> Yet I will defend my ways to his face . . .
> Job 13:15

Job's dialogue with his friends continues throughout most of the book, and in the course of it, they cover just about every rational explanation that can be advanced for human suffering. Suddenly, another Person enters the conversation. A storm springs up, and "the Lord answered Job out of the whirlwind."

If you approach this dramatic climax expecting God to offer an eloquent, logical defense of His justice, you'll be greatly disappointed. "The issue, as Job had posed it, is completely ignored," says Pope. "No explanation or excuse is offered for Job's suffering. As Job had expected, God refuses to submit to questioning. But, contrary to expectation, God does not crush him, or brush him away, or multiply his wounds." What God does is to ask Job some questions of His own:

> Where were you when I laid the foundations of the
> earth? . . . Have the gates of death been revealed

to you, or have you seen the gates of deep darkness?
. . . Can you bind the chains of the Pleiades, or loose
the cords of Orion? . . . Is it by your wisdom that
the hawk soars, and spreads his wings toward the
south?

Job 38, 39

The net effect of the divine discourse, which continues
through four chapters of magnificent poetry, is to con-
vince Job that it is impossible for finite human understanding to comprehend the ways of One who is the Author
not only of the universe, but also of the concept of justice.

Job is completely satisfied with this answer. Indeed, the
most profound point of the story is that when Job encounters the Living God in person, he loses all interest in abstract arguments about God's justice, mercy, or other attributes. He is so enraptured by the Reality that he ceases
to care about theory.

"I have uttered what I did not understand, things too
wonderful for me, which I did not know," Job confesses
in the final chapter. "I had heard of thee by the hearing
of the ear, but now my eye sees thee; therefore I despise
myself, and repent in dust and ashes."

But God's wrath is directed not against Job, who cared
enough to ask the deep dark questions, but against the
three pious "comforters" who offered glib and superficial
answers. "My wrath is kindled against you," He tells them,
"for you have not spoken of me what is right, as my servant Job has."

In other words, God does not expect men to kid themselves—or others—about the existence of evil, pain, and
suffering in the world, or about the fact that great misfortunes sometimes befall righteous people, while blatant
sinners enjoy prosperity and popular adulation. That *is*

the way of the world, and if anyone needs any further proof of it, he has only to consider what happened to Jesus of Nazareth. The Crucifixion is the New Testament seal on Job's contention that the innocent do suffer. And the Resurrection gives to all men the assurance which the Voice from the whirlwind gave to Job: no matter how baffling and confusing life may be, no matter how clearly evil may seem to have triumphed, God remains sovereign and men can safely trust their ultimate destinies to his often-inscrutable but ever-merciful Will.

When you get right down to it, the only answer to the problem of evil is the *experience* of God's nearness and providential care that comes from a life of faith. But that has been a sufficient answer for everyone who has really tried it.

The author of this Biblical masterpiece is unknown to us. Nor is there any consensus among Biblical scholars about its probable date. Guesses range all the way from 2000 B.C.—the age of the Patriarchs—to 300 B.C. One plausible thesis, which bears the imprimatur of the great W. F. Albright, is that the book was written about the sixth century B.C., and that it incorporates (primarily in its prose prologue and epilogue) a folk story that had been circulated in Israel for a thousand years or more.

You don't need to read all forty-two chapters to get the meat of the story. In fact, I think you'll get more out of it if you do skip over a large interior segment in which the arguments between Job and his comforters are repeated for a second and then a third time without any significant new ideas being introduced. It also is desirable to skip the long-winded speeches of a pompous young ass named Elihu who pops up out of nowhere in chapter 32 to set Job straight. Elihu probably is an editorial interpolation by a later writer. He adds nothing worthwhile to the story, and delays the dramatic climax in which Job is answered by God out of the storm.

To get down to specifics, the reading plan I recommend is: read chapters 1 through 14, skip to chapter 19 (which contains one of Job's best speeches), then skip again to chapter 38, where begins the divine answer. Read straight on through to the end (chapter 42).

VIII

THE PSALMS

When we embarked on this Bible-reading plan, I said that if you were going to read only one book of the Bible, it should be Luke's gospel. Now, at the end, I can add that if you were going to read only *two* books of the Bible, I would unhesitatingly recommend that the second one be the PSALMS.

I've saved them for last because if anything can make an habitual Bible reader out of you, the Psalms can. Here is a part of the Bible you can read over and over again, and where you will always find new treasures. More than any other part of the Bible, the Psalms are meant to be read devotionally. Nothing will enrich your spiritual life more than the habit of reading one psalm a day, as an integral part of your period of private prayer and meditation.

Many psalms *are* prayers in effect, although technically all are songs which were originally meant to be sung aloud to the accompaniment of stringed instruments. Of the thousands of such songs, composed by various poets and musicians during the long history of Israel, one hundred and fifty have been preserved in the Old Testament book of Psalms or, as our ancestors called it, the Psalter.[*]

According to Hebrew literary convention, psalms are attributed to David as wisdom books are attributed to Solomon. You'll find that seventy-three of the Old Testament psalms are designated in the Biblical text as having been composed by David. Until recently, modern scholarship tended to assume that most if not all psalms were written long after David's time. But this view has lately undergone re-examination, and the best authorities are now saying that it is not only possible, but quite likely that a fair number of them, including Psalms 2, 16, 28, 29, 40, 48, 82, 108, and 110, were actually composed during David's reign. There seems to be no good reason for doubting that the musician-king himself was responsible for some of them.

Who wrote a particular psalm is of small importance in any case. All Hebrews had a share in the production of this priceless library of sacred songs—their common experience of life and worship of God is reflected in them.

When you consider what enormous differences of language, culture, cosmology, and civilization separate our

---

[*] Another collection of ancient psalms turned up recently among the Dead Sea Scrolls. Others may be found as the recovery of old Hebrew libraries continues.

world from that of the ancient Hebrews, it is somewhat awesome that their songs are still being used in public worship as well as private devotions, not only by Jews, but also by Protestants, Catholics, and Eastern Orthodox Christians. One of the really important things that all branches of the Judeo-Christian family have in common is the custom of reciting psalms at every regular worship service as well as at special occasions such as weddings, funerals, baptisms, and bar mitzvahs.

Christians have sometimes tended to forget, or minimize, their great debt to the Hebrew heritage represented by the Old Testament prophets. But they have always cherished the Psalms. The first Christian martyrs went to their deaths in the Roman Coliseum singing psalms. Martin Luther preferred his "old and ragged Psalter" to all other books of the Bible. One of the first books printed in America was a translation of the Psalms made and used by the Puritans of the Massachusetts Bay Colony.*

In attaching great value to Psalms, Christians are simply following Jesus' example. He frequently quoted Psalms in his teaching, and in his final agony on the cross, recited a verse from Psalm 22: "My God, my God, why hast thou forsaken me?"

The perennial power of Psalms is due, in part, to the fact that they cover the whole range of human emotions. No matter what mood you are in, or what feeling you need to express, you can find a psalm that fits it.

Suppose, for example, that you are going through one of those "dark nights of the soul" when nothing good seems real and God seems far away. The author of Psalm 63 felt the same way when he cried:

---

* Only a few copies of this 1640 *Bay Psalm Book* have survived, and each of them is worth a fortune today on the rare-book market.

O God, thou art my God, I seek thee,
my soul thirsts for thee;
my flesh faints for thee,
    as in a dry and weary land where no water is.

Or, to move to the other end of the emotional scale, suppose you are standing outdoors on a starlit night and your heart suddenly leaps with wonder at the vastness of the universe. Psalm 8 says it for you:

When I look at thy heavens, the work of thy fingers,
the moon and the stars which thou hast established;
what is man that thou art mindful of him,
    and the son of man that thou dost care for him?

In time of illness or distress, you may find a ready-made prayer in Psalm 102:

Hear my prayer, O Lord;
let my cry come to thee!
Do not hide thy face from me
    in the day of my distress!
Incline thy ear to me;
    answer me speedily in the day when I call!

For my days pass away like smoke,
    and my bones burn like a furnace.
My heart is smitten like grass, and withered;
    I forget to eat my bread.
Because of my loud groaning
    my bones cleave to my flesh.

Or perhaps you have been delivered from great trouble, and your inhibited twentieth-century heart needs the help of the author of Psalm 18 to express what you feel:

I love thee, O Lord, my strength.
The Lord is my rock, and my fortress, and my deliverer,
    my God, my rock, in whom I take refuge,
    my shield, and the horn of my salvation, my strong-
        hold.

There are even psalms which vividly express such un-
worthy but all-too-human emotions as the desire for revenge against enemies. You could hardly ask for a more
bloodthirsty prayer than the one you'll find in Psalm 58:

O God, break the teeth in their mouths;
    tear out the fangs of the young lions, O Lord!
Let them vanish like water that runs away;
    like grass let them be trodden down and wither.
Let them be like the snail which dissolves into slime,
    like the untimely birth that never sees the sun.

You will want to read all the Psalms, from the first right
through the one hundred and fiftieth. It is a good idea to
mark your favorites as you go through, and jot a word or
two in the margin about the dominant theme.

Sometimes, of course, a single psalm may touch on several different themes. In that case, you can put an identi-
fying tag on each passage that especially appeals to you.

AN INDEX OF PSALMS

Although I hope you'll make your own informal index
to the Psalms, here is one—very incomplete and admittedly open to argument at many points—to which you can
refer if you find yourself urgently needing an appropriate
psalm before you've had a chance to read through the
whole book.

Psalms of praise and adoration (the highest and most important type of prayer, and the one which most of us tend to neglect without the help of some devotional aid such as the Psalms):

2d
8th
18th
19th (exceptionally fine)
24th
29th
42d
48th
50th
63d
65th
66th
76th
81st
84th
89th
90th (perhaps the greatest of all psalms)
93d
113th
115th
135th
139th (very, very good)
145th (another great one)
146th
147th
148th
149th
150th

Psalms of thanksgiving and trust (another kind of prayer that we often neglect):

3d
4th
5th
9th
16th
18th
23d (everybody's favorite)
27th
30th
34th
40th
46th (very good)
62d
75th
91st
92d (also very good)
95th (source of the Venite)
96th
100th (widely used in liturgical worship)
103d (right out of the top drawer)
121st
136th

Psalms of repentance:

6th
25th
38th
51st (much the best in this category)
79th

Pleas for help or deliverance from troubles:

        7th
        12th
        13th
        17th
        20th
        22d (the one Jesus used on the Cross)
        28th
        31st
        42d
        43d
        44th
        55th
        57th
        61st
        69th (highly recommended)
        70th
        71st (excellent)
        77th
        88th
        102d (the sick man's prayer)
        130th (one of the very best)
        140th
        141st
        142d
        143d

A prayer for brotherhood and unity:

        133d

A song of pure joy:

        108th

A FINAL WORD

If you're still with me at this point, and have worked your way through the entire reading plan outlined in the preceding chapters, you can now award yourself a diploma. You may once have considered yourself a Biblical illiterate, but you are now a bona-fide Bible reader. Only a small proportion of church members, perhaps fewer than ten per cent, are as familiar with the Bible as you are.

But that doesn't mean you can now put your Bible away and forget about it. It is one of the noteworthy characteristics of the Bible that it rewards rereading. You nearly always learn more on your second or third reading of any particular book than you learned on the first reading. Now that you've gotten acquainted with your Bible, let it become your lifetime companion. There will be, even now, times when it will baffle or bore you. But if you stay with it, it will be an open channel through which God can speak to you.

What more can you ask of a book?

OTHER BOOKS TO READ

Thousands of books have been written about the Bible. Some are highly technical and abstruse, written by scholars for scholars. Others are "popular" at a banal level that insults the intelligence of the educated laymen. A few combine sound scholarship with lucid literary style.

For reference purposes—if you want to find out more about the historical background, language, and probable meaning of a particular passage of Scripture or about a person, event, or concept of the Bible—your best bet is to go to a church or public library, and seek out one of the following:

The Interpreter's Bible (12 vols.; Nashville: Abingdon-Cokesbury, 1951–57)

The Interpreter's Dictionary of the Bible (4 vols.; Nashville: Abingdon, 1962)

The Anchor Bible (36 vols.; New York: Doubleday, 1964 ff.)

The Abingdon Bible Commentary (1 vol.; Nashville: Abingdon, 1929)

If you'd like to delve more deeply into what scholars call *hermeneutics*—that is, how the Bible is to be read and interpreted—I would commend the following to your attention:

Conversation with the Bible by Markus Barth (New York: Holt, Rinehart & Winston, 1964)

Invitation to the New Testament by W. D. Davies (New York: Doubleday, 1966)

The Bible Speaks to You by Robert McAfee Brown (Philadelphia: Westminster, 1955)

Searching the Scriptures by John J. Dougherty (New York: Doubleday, 1959)

How to Read the Bible by Frederick C. Grant (New York: Collier, 1962)

A Short History of the Interpretation of the Bible by Robert M. Grant (New York: Macmillan, 1963)

As a guide to the literary treasures of the Bible, you can't beat Mary Ellen Chase's classic *The Bible and the Common Reader* (published by Macmillan, 1944; rev. ed., 1952). Any library worthy of the name should have it.

INDEX